Rethinking Sartre

A Political Reading

John C. Carney

UNIVERSITY PRESS OF AMERICA,® INC.
Lanham • Boulder • New York • Toronto • Plymouth, UK

Copyright © 2007 by
University Press of America,® Inc.
4501 Forbes Boulevard
Suite 200
Lanham, Maryland 20706
UPA Acquisitions Department (301) 459-3366

Estover Road
Plymouth PL6 7PY
United Kingdom

Library of Congress Control Number: 2007920780
ISBN-13: 978-0-7618-3688-9 (paperback : alk. paper)
ISBN-10: 0-7618-3688-8 (paperback : alk. paper)

∞™ The paper used in this publication meets the minimum
requirements of American National Standard for Information
Sciences—Permanence of Paper for Printed Library Materials,
ANSI/NISO Z39.48-1992.

To Patty

Contents

Acknowledgments

I would like to acknowledge Patricia Misciagno for her support in the writing of this book. It was my dear friend Patty who suggested that I attend the Graduate Faculty years ago. Patricia's own contribution to philosophy has had a profound influence on my own approach to philosophy.

I would also like to thank my extraordinarily talented friend Vincent Amato for his encouragement and for many wonderful conversations about the relationship between religion and philosophy. As a gifted writer photographer and scholar, Vince's suggestions were both timely and insightful. I would also like to thank my dear friend Dean Joel Kassiola of San Francisco State University for his encouragement over the years. In addition I would like to acknowledge the support of Professor Robert Scharff of the University of New Hampshire for sharing his insights into phenomenology and for his wit and support. My former student and friend Jonathan Shoemaker of the Graduate Philosophy Program at Claremont University has been more than generous with his own thinking on these matters. I have been fortunate to have had many truly gifted students over the years at Manhattanville College and other universities. I am deeply grateful to all of them for the depth and authenticity of their thinking. I am grateful to the Manhattanville College community for its support. I would also like to thank my friend Dr. Antonio Leopold Rappa of National University of Singapore for sharing his remembrances of Henry S. Kariel's philosophy. Finally, I would like to thank the people at University Press of America and in particular David Chao and Patti Belcher for their help in bringing this project to publication.

Chapter One

Rethinking Sartre

A few years ago I was teaching at a state university that had a number of satellite campuses and at these satellite campuses this particular university used video tapes of various professors for some of their courses instead of actual live professors. More often than not as I walked to my classroom I would pass by one of the rooms wherein the video was playing, often blaring in a room with nobody in it. Occasionally a bored student would be there, slumped over a chair, pen just barely in their hand and looking as though they had been drugged. One evening as I passed the professor on the monitor, I noticed that it was a psychologist speaking about existentialism and the existentialism of Jean-Paul Sartre at that. I stopped and listened as he proceeded to give what has become now a fairly common portrayal of Sartre's philosophy. Have you heard it? In this view Sartre is the advocate for a "pull-yourself-up-by-your-own-bootstraps" philosophy in which there is a great deal of hand-wringing and lots and lots of loneliness. Oddly enough, the setting for this account of Sartre's philosophy couldn't have been more apt as it recalled for me the famous scene from one of his late plays, <u>The Condemned of Altona</u> where a giant T.V. just like the one in the room I just passed, blares away in a final indictment, an endnote if you will, of the absurdity of bad faith. If this were not actually so serious a disservice, first to the students who have to endure such treatment and then to the actual philosophy that Sartre worked to present, this view of Sartre's work, caricature that it is, would have been merely one more episode along the way in academia. It has however become far more widespread than students of Sartre might be aware and it rests on some interpretations of Sartre's work that have become fairly well entrenched. The reason for this perhaps owes to the fact that Sartre's work is so accessible that it can seem to stand alone without the heavy lifting entailed by carefully explaining some of his core concepts such as the concept of intentionality. Recent works on Sartre have not helped matters much. For example Bernard Levy's recent study of Sartre contains barely any mention of his concept of intentionality at all, devoting only two pages of a book that spans hundreds and hundreds of pages. When he does get around to discussing it Levy locates it in the context of a disagreement between Sartre and certain famous authors such as Dos Pasos and Faulkner.[1] Yet for Sartre the whole point of the concept of intentionality was its realism and so the mistake here is that of using aesthetics as the basis for intentionality thus denuding intentionality of its connection to direct realism, an essential aspect of Sartre's philosophy. But perhaps an even more egregious mistake in Levy's approach is the overemphasis that he places on the philosophy of Henri Bergson.[2] It is not so much that Bergson's work did not enjoy great influence on Sartre generally, since all of France was enthralled by his works, but that Bergson's approach, especially in *Matter and Memory* is thoroughly metaphysical whereas an accurate subtitle to the totality of Sartre's philosophy might read: *Phenomenology Against Metaphysics*. The effect is to remove the political dimension from Sartre's philosophy and reduce its philosophical weight to the pronouncements that Sartre made on this or that issue of current affairs. In addition to Levy's work there has also appeared a number of biographies some short and some that are truly voluminous. With these works there is on the one hand a tendency to focus far too much on Sartre's personal limitations or else to treat him like a cult figure and yet once again the result is to remove from view the truly significant aspect of his work, his actual philosophy itself.

An additional reason for the diminution of his work is that it can in certain superficial ways be made to appear like some of the fad philosophies that have seemed to proliferate in recent years. Here a kind of "my Sartre" has taken root and one finds in Sartre whatever one may have wished to find in their favorite pop psychology or philosophy. Thus for the devotees of Ayn Rand there is a Sartrean twist, or else Sartre is an early proponent for a kind of neo-liberalism that is deeply suspicious of any group or social action. For example, Andrew Leak, in his work on Sartre declares that Sartre declined after 1960 having been eclipsed by those in the structuralist school.[3] Leak argues that Sartre had a standard answer for any form of the structuralist point of view in which Sartre invokes praxis as the more essential concept. Yet, the irony here is that Sartre's influence by way of the concept of *praxis*, which began with *Search for a Method*, had an immediate and widespread influence that informed so much of European politics during the 1960s and even thereafter. In fact, many of the debates over structuralism well into the 80s evinced remnants of Sartre's earlier critique of it. It is hard to believe that one recent author actually criticizes Sartre for not having responded in greater detail to the structural argument when such large sections of the *Critique of Dialecti-*

cal Reason are devoted to it. For example, in one section of the Critique Sartre discusses the influence of the structure of a academic schedule on the learning experience of students. Sartre notes, "There can in fact be no doubt that reciprocal relations can be treated by the 'exact sciences': and they are already present, as a foundation, in the administration of a school when it decides the timetable for a particular class or in the strict arrangement of the train timetable of a particular network for the winter or summer period. But, on the other hand, it should be noticed that these calculated determinations nevertheless refer to actions. Thus the peculiarity of this 'ossature' seems to be that it is both an inert relation and a living praxis. After writing so many critiques and notations to structuralism one would have to ask in Sartre's defense what else actually remains to be said. The fact is one could not ask for more from a philosophical exposition of a position, for Sartre is quite careful in his use of language, he takes pains to define his points and provides painstaking amounts of evidence with ample demonstrations of all of his concepts. So may of the critiques of his work seem to have left-handed compliments but fail to provide the greatest compliment—an accurate presentation of his philosophy.

Another point that should be noted concerns Sartre's lifelong revulsion of racism and its many institutional forms including that of colonialism and neo-colonialism. This topic, when seen in retrospect would seem to place him in far more unique company in the history of philosophy than is generally considered to be the case. The radical position that he occupied seems to have been lost in the overall hurry to revise the history of the latter part of the Twentieth-Century according to which there was such "universal" opposition to the wars in Algeria and Vietnam. Sartre's radicalism has also been eclipsed by his investiture in the culture of celebrity where one, but merely one of many expressions is the near-obsessive concern with his relationship to Simone de Beauvoir, an obsession that has the effect of excluding the political implications of what Sartre actually wrote.[4] Obviously Sartre's actual philosophical contribution is the essential aspect and not these various trivialities from his personal life. But even in terms of his contribution to the study of politics there has been an overemphasis on his opinions over his actual philosophical works. Here, the point is that as important as Sartre's insights into various schools of thought may be, and as interesting as his personal politics may have been, the real story of Sartre's critique of politics is one that is unique and in many ways has yet to be told. In fact, what is far useful for political theory and what is a good deal more profound for philosophy than even his analysis and specific engagements in the political world are the force of his concepts when they are placed in the context of the doctrine of intentionality. For one thing, such a focus allows one to avoid the tendency, so widespread today, of succumbing to the fallacy whereby Sartre's personality with all of its limitations, becomes the filter though which his philosophy is assessed. Philosophy has traditionally assigned the label of "fallacy" to such attempts to avoid the actual issues a philosopher raises but in the case of Sartre this is a particularly infelicitous. It has to do with the vantage point that Sartre advocates for in that by focusing on Sartre and making that the vantage point what is lost sight of is the actual vantage point he proposes, that of being-in-the-world. It is this unique vantage point, explained through the use of the concept of intentionality that serves as the basis for the critique of ideology that can be deduced from Sartre's philosophy. Looking at the world from the vantage point of being-in-the-world, as explicated by the idea of intentionality, exposes ideology immediately for what it is even while positively establishing what actually is the case in any given instance. Describing the intentional structure of experience as Sartre does at the same time to highlights all of the attempts undertaken through bad faith to present a mediated view of the human condition. Here, bad faith offers the temptation to use ideology as a means of hiding politics behind a timeless depiction of human nature.

What is proposed in this work is something of an alternative approach but it is one that has generated some of truly remarkable works on Sartre like that of McBride, Flynn and more recently McCulloch where there is a sustained focus on the concepts that Sartre used to present his philosophy and to have these serve as the guide for interpreting his philosophy. The most essential of these is Sartre's concept of intentionality and so this work will proceed to explain the concept and how it remained the focal point for Sartre's philosophy from his early works to his latest. One thing that becomes fairly obvious when this approach is taken is that Sartre's philosophy has a great deal more continuity than it appears to have when the concept of intentionality recedes into the background or even into obscurity. It also helps to shed light on the power of Sartre's work to critique and explicate all manifestations of ideology. This work argues that it is chiefly this, the power of his critique of ideology that represents Sartre's greatest political legacy. In terms of critiquing ideology, it seems to have been Sartre's focus early on since in his autobiography he recalls instances where certain elitist fellow students were persuaded by the power of Nietzsche's thought to make it their ideology, a development Sartre even at an early age took exception to. On the other hand, the earlier-noted work, *the Condemned of Altona,* a fairly late work, is a sustained critique of the ideology of exceptionalism that is so deeply rooted in the perpetuation of bad faith.

Perhaps nowhere is the tendency to engage in bad faith as politics more pronounced than in the example of essentialism. Sartre's work has traditionally been presented as an antidote to this form of ideology wherein this or that view of human nature is imposed on all humanity. Viewed in hindsight one would have to agree with Sartre in focusing on the critique of human nature. For more than anything else it is essentialism that serves as the lynchpin for the most virulent political ideologies and ideologies of all sorts. In fact, one of the reasons why a rethinking of Sartre is necessary today is that many of his most important arguments are based on his concept of intentionality and this concept has receded in recent years for the reasons noted above. At the same time a new form of essentialism has emerged and along with it new ideologies such as that of Neoliberalism and these are in serious need of critique from the point of view of Sartre's phenomenology. Essentialism always entails claims regarding human nature and by implication, posits a view that human beings do not change. As its devotees have learned, one could simply not ask for more from an ideology of quietism and it is for this reason that essentialism has grown in such popularity in recent years. After all, why bother to enact positive public policy when after all, people will merely be what they currently are—it is "human nature" to behave so. However, the current form of essentialism is somewhat different than in the past and so it may be useful to say a word about it before proceeding. For the reader needs to only ask if Harvey Mansfield's book *Manliness* or any of the many other ideological tomes to appear in recent years could possibly have been written without an unacknowledged reliance on a static notion of the individual. Sometimes in these works change will be included in one of these arguments, but then it is merely to reaffirm the same old essentialist and static claims about individuals, as for example in Dinesh D'Souza's work. Because it is such an important but as noted unacknowledged feature of contemporary ideological claims, it may be useful to say some more about current forms of essentialism.

THE NEW ESSENTIALISM

For many observers the end of the cold war promised an end to ideology but the regrettable fact is that even more than ever our age seems to be one of extreme ideology. The reemergence of essentialist claims about the individual has a great deal to do with this. Essentialism is form of reification in which attributes of historical beings, human beings, are fostered onto an abstract, ahistorical individual who is then used as the template for all of humanity or, in some instances, is subdivided among categories such as nation, race or gender. Contemporary media culture has reinforced these pseudo-universal statements and one need not look very far to see the evidence for this. The way this works is as follows: On the issue of class and wealth media culture has come to be defined by obsequious attention to celebrity wherein the *demi*-gods that C. Wright Mills identified as the *power elite*, are celebrated as the exemplars of the corporate attributes which they are depicted as possessing as an essential part of their personality. Here, instead of the analysis of wealth in America there is an almost cult-like attention afforded to captains of industry, so much so that members of the once-proud profession of news reporting, a profession that in areas removed from wealth and class continues to often evince high standards, are reduced to waiting in attendance on every word that the captains will offer.[5] Their treatment of wealth in America includes the virtues they promote—a kind of cut-throat materialism that often leaves human wreckage in its wake. The perpetrators are then celebrated for their alleged essentialist qualities, their aggression, their ability to "make tough decisions" like firing workers or outsourcing thousands of jobs, and other "manly" qualities.

The new essentialism has emerged as a serious problem of political theory once again because it has disappeared from debate even while continuing to inform public discourse about politics at every level. One can see it in the disturbing idol worship that citizens display to these "fortunate" possessors of these traits. What can serve as a greater reminder of the force of alienation than the sight of members of the working class seeing to acquire these essential traits through each and every new consumer product that is marketed as a magic elixir that will make them, somehow, members of the power elite too. Expressions of idol worship become ideology when individuals become alienated from the initial source of the privileged status accorded to celebrity or the accoutrements of consumer society. That source is human agency itself, or the capacity of one to act and to create things including values. However, if one reflects on the relationship between contemporary idol worship, reification and the ideology that it generates, it seems as though the lynchpin for all of this is something more pernicious still, that of the idolizing of the human subject. For the problem facing contemporary America and increasingly the rest of the world as well, is not merely that the subject has been reduced to a consumer, a deformed expression of human existence, but rather that, when seen in the light of Sartre's philosophy, the subject has first of all been afforded greater importance than human existence itself. It is the latter which is the actual basis of all that essentialism of every age says that it celebrates: human dignity, freedom, creativity, passion, and human reason itself. For to say that human existence is prior to the subject is to say that there is something deeper in human existence than the various roles and sets of assumptions that are offered in its place. It is to locate human dignity in the intentional structure of existence and to see in it the full measure of human freedom and passion and not some lesser imitation.[6] It is a measure of the current state of theory that mistaking the two, or viewing them as synonymous, which is tantamount to essentialism, has become almost axiomatic even within philosophy, including political philosophy.

As the reader may have judged from these initial remarks, this work is a critique of the politics of essentialism on the basis of an argument put forth by Jean-Paul Sartre which, if true is a powerful counter-example to the basic point of the new essentialism. Before proceeding to present that argument, it may be useful to say a few words about the new essentialism. From a philosophical point of view the new essentialism argues that there are in fact fundamental differences among individuals that are fixed and that operate in individual lives and historically as a structure that reappears under various forms, all of which share this in common – that all such manifestations can be reduced to these core distinctions and essences. The most widespread example of this approach to human existence is perhaps that of an essential difference that is said to inform the experience of being male or female. Thus, for proponents of this approach it may be true or not that the meaning of "man" and "woman" is socially constructed; there is a discernable, verifiable difference, an essence, if one prefers, between male and female. But the by now familiar debate over essentialism and difference that has informed so much of political theory, especially feminist political theory in the last fifty years is but one manifestation of essentialism or the debate over essentialism. That debate has now been joined and augmented by new research, especially in the fields of psychology and sociology, which have come to rely on findings in the biological sciences to help establish their claims about in inherent, or essential differences.

These claims are not new of course, but what makes them somewhat different is the above-noted reliance on new findings in the biological sciences and medical research, including the harnessing of advanced technology to "prove" these differences are "naturalized" as essential. We are in different philosophical terrain when we begin to posit essential differences on the basis of the new research, for it is not so much a matter of "nature" versus "nurture" that is at issue, as it is a depiction of the foundations of human existence. So while it appears that the new essentialism is making scientific claims about aspects of human existence, in fact the residue that is advanced is a claim about human existence as biologically based and more or less immutable. Thus, while individuals may wage a "white knuckled" effort against male aggression, it is just that for one is truly going against the tide of human nature. Under the guise of the new essentialism all kinds of justifications have been advanced for everything from a plea for more manly men to apologetics for authoritarian regimes in developing countries.

The view annunciated here is that Sartre's argument against essentialism old and new is a kind of reality therapy for our age. The arguments are powerful and evidence-based and offer a powerful counter-example to the universal statements that come from the new essentialist theorists and researchers. The first distinction that should probably be made is the one between science and the ideology of science, or the new essentialism. The first has been the basis of human advancement and has led to the enrichment of the quality of human life from the outset. The latter offers nothing to science itself but is used as an ideological bat to fend off, in some instances actual scientific advances. More than that though, it has provided ideological cover for some of the most anti-humanitarian politics and policies afoot in the world today. There is in fact a kind of sleight of hand that is at the core of the new essentialism because at least part of the reason why this new essentialism has become so powerful is that it has been accompanied by truly breathtaking developments in the biological sciences. For we live in an engineered age: Everything from one's appearance to the outside world, to one's moods and even the food we eat has been designed.

One of the characteristics that help to distinguish Sartre's approach from that of others is his insistence on viewing epistemology as a political category, and thus one that deserves the same critical perspectives as other theoretical claims. This was a lifelong perspective on the part of Sartre for, as this work notes, one of Sartre's very first philosophical works was a critical essay on the epistemology of Edmund Husserl's new approach to philosophy, that of phenomenology. On this topic it is worth pointing out that Sartre insistence on the political character of epistemology has an important allay in the late physicist Paul Feyerabend. For Feyerabend too, the free pass that is sometimes given to inquiry as such has often generated the most persistent untruths and these sometimes eventually passes into tradition as an immovable orthodoxy that works against the practice of analysis.[7] The question arises therefore, if actual science is existential, whereas its ideology is essentialist; might not the actual philosophy of science be existential and non-essentialist itself?

Another way of approaching this is to say that Sartre's phenomenology is such that its existentialism resides not only in the arguments that it advances about the human condition but also includes its epistemology. Sartre's approach is therefore a truly critical one in that he insists that the nomenclature and procedures one uses to analyze one's topics be subjected to the same critical gaze as other components of philosophy. This was the basis, after all, of his early critique of no less a figure than Husserl. In fact, more than most other philosophies Sartre's approach stands in sharpest contest to the universal claims at the center on the new essentialism. On this topic, it may useful to say a bit more about the new essentialism because this will serve to place Sartre's phenomenology generally, and the specific keystone for this study, his doctrine of intentionality, in an historical context as truly critical philosophy.

THE PROBLEMS OF ABSTRACTION AND *AHISTORICAL* REASON IN THE NEW ESSENTIALISM.

It is important to begin by distinguishing older forms of essentialism from more recent expressions, and on this topic it seems clear that while both the old and the new essentialism are deeply imbued in theories of human nature, current forms of essentialism involve extensions from research in the biological sciences to new fields and disciplines in specifically ideological ways. Previous instances of essentialism were invariably religiously based, as for example one finds in the arguments of the Nineteenth-Century opponents to women's suffrage. Furthermore, the old essentialism made use of scientific research primarily to reinforce its ideology and its own traditional philosophies of human nature. The new essentialism has refined the universalizing tendencies of the older versions in order to take account of new political realities. For example, whereas the old essentialism was content to make fundamental claims about human nature and to allow the category of human nature to serve as a terminus for whatever could not, or dare not be explained by science, the new essentialism posits claims about human nature immanently. Thus, not only are the categories "man" and "woman" essentialized relative to one another, but there is also an immanent argument which posits that all men and all women, as such, are alike. In fact, the category of man and woman is increasingly expanded to include the class of all primates. The end result, as noted above is a reinforcement of a political discourse of fatalism wherein the subtext is that politics and praxis amount to really nothing so much as tinkering around the margins; since fundamental causality resides at the genetic level.

However, there is an extremely important contradiction in the new essentialism and it is one that the old essentialism did not have to concern itself with at all. For when we speak of a human essence or a set of essences we are by definition making a claim that something does not change; since as essence it defines the class. However technology has increasingly placed the agency over these alleged essences in the hands of individuals and so it is a contradiction to argue that there is an essential meaning to the category "man" or "woman," when that status can be changed by individual fiat or agency. Of course, it could be argued that such changes leave intact the actual essence according to which, for example, the ability to have children defines a woman, and the ability to father children defines a man, or some other similar definition. But here again we are once again back in the same morass of arbitrary definitions and universal statements, each of which can be disproved by the numerous counter-examples that have proliferated under the new genetic engineering. So in a sense the actual practice of science has outpaced the ideology of science and that consequently, it is Sartre who actually has the correct interpretation of the human condition – that freedom is the human being's only essence.

An additional distinguishing feature of the new essentialism is that its ideology lacks the mediation of philosophies of human nature. This is in part due to the historical emergence of new social movements and as a result the new essentialism extends its arguments from fragments of the research itself. Thus, ideological claims are made that extend well beyond the narrow scope of research and eventually surface in the political realm where they inform the political world. The debate and the resulting electoral victory of the Republican party in the 2004 election is generally considered to have been won on the basis of just such ideologies of human nature on issues such as gay marriage and stem-cell research.

One question that emerges at this point is that of how to think about genetic predisposition and other aspects of contemporary research. Looking at these proclivities and predispositions does not imply their outright denial of course but only their status as an essence. So the question is really an archeo-philosophical one— how did these traits that have been depicted as essences came to be. In this context Sartre follows Rousseau but in a radically new key he offers a compelling account that transcends Rousseau's argument in the Social Contract and instead introduces a radical theory of history. In his later account *The Critique of Dialectical Reason* Sartre demonstrates how the condition of "scarcity" and the need to overcome it through praxis generates human capabilities and skills that are often mistaken for a fixed human essence. Arguably it is here more than anywhere else that we begin to see the significance of Sartre's insistence on viewing epistemology as a political category. For, his analysis helps to shed light, by contrast as well as argumentation, on the theoretical problem of abstraction that is especially prevalent in essentialist thought. In his analysis of the ideology of epistemology and the "everyday" Sartre identifies two aspects of abstraction that necessitate specific attention. The first is the tendency of ideologies to abstract historically situated behaviors and to present them as timeless, a strong component of Sartre's early works, including his literary ones. The second involves the ideological depiction of history itself the focus of Sartre's later philosophy. In this context it is the searing critique of ideological accounts of history that he discusses in the *Critique of Dialectical Reason* that is the most astute. However, the argument of the Critique relies on the fundamental claim that Sartre makes early on about the intentional structure of human experience.[8]

Another hallmark of the new essentialism is its penchant for making claims of human nature terminate in the genetic code. So if one is a diabetic or suffers any number of psychological maladies it is sure to be the case that the cause for this will be one's genetic makeup. Viewed from the perspective of contemporary political psychology, it is as though Piaget never existed.

Sartre departs from most of these approaches, especially ones that view the subject in an ahistorical way in that he insists that true human dignity is found in the primordial capacity of human beings to exercise their agency and to relate to the world, and so one way to say this is to reflect on the fact that Sartre's existentialism has draw criticism from both old detractors and new. Many of these detractors are in the essentialist school and direct their displeasure at Sartre and his partner Simone de Beauvoir more than anyone else. And, for good reason since Sartre's existentialism will rain on one's theoretical parade whether it is a plea for manly men that one has nostalgically in mind, or the category woman depicted as an essence that one wishes to celebrate.

The truth is that the existentialism of Sartre has only infrequently been given its full measure. Often his philosophy is depicted as a philosophy of choice as though Sartre were arguing for freedom of the will, a position he lampooned and critiqued whenever possible. His actual philosophy rests on his interpretation of the concept on intentionality which is one of the finest arguments ever advanced and that, when fully developed is more than up to the challenges that have been leveled against it. It should also be said that few philosophies have had such diverse opponents as has Sartre. For example, in her critical analysis of Sartre's work, Rosemary Tong neglects to mention that for Sartre the whole point of existentialism is the presence of human freedom *prior to the subject*.[9] Similarly, Stern's analysis which places Sartre in the camp with psychoanalyst Alfred Adler also neglects that it is the critique of the subject that is the often unacknowledged basis of his critique of Freud. Psychologists have often found in Sartre a proponent of a "pull-yourself-up-by-your-own-bootstraps" paradigm when, in fact, nothing could be further from the truth. The intentional structure of human existence is not by any stretch a guide for self-help.

THE NEW ESSENTIALISM OF THE LEFT:
A WORD ON HUMAN SEXUALITY

If the new essentialism of the Right involves ahistorical reason in search of a static human nature; the new essentialism of the Left posits the idea that human sexuality provides the basis for establishing multiple identities. Here the fundamental idea is that an anthropological account of human existence evinces our similarity with other biological species which present a consistent and stable set of relationships and structures. These structures therefore, must be taken as evidence of a more basic essence structured along the lines of innate predispositions and biology. For example, in one study that has been widely cited, a biological root of homosexuality among males is traced to birth order. Here, the research is alleged to indicate that the youngest of a series of brothers is more likely to by homosexual. This was of course immediately seized upon by those with a political interest in the public policy of gender issues to argue that such a biological condition is beyond human agency. It may be true of course that such a position would make good public policy, but it is awful philosophy and even worse political philosophy. The merits of public policy debates should stand or fall on the basis of its politics and not an alleged apolitical epistemology. This is because what is entailed by this essentialized epistemology is far worse in terms of eventual public policy, let alone philosophy than any actually existing political condition.[10]

By contrast, rethinking Sartre from the perspective of human sexuality leads one to pose some very disruptive questions for Left essentialism. For one thing, Sartre is one of the few philosophers to actually address the issue of human sexuality directly. When he does so, especially in the course of his critique of empirical psychology, he makes the case that sexuality of itself does not deserve to be privileged over other facets of human passion. Instead, he asks us to consider why this is so and if it is not more persuasive to hold that the libido itself is based on something more basic still—our ability to enter into relationships *per se*.So in other words, if the libido is not the most primary structure of human experience then human sexuality, by definition, is not either. From the perspective of Sartre's concept of intentionality, if this is the case than the discourse over multiple identities and so forth is also called into question. Here too though, the tendency of human reason to essentialize categories, even that of human sexuality, for ideological purposes is pervasive. Here the argument is that there is an innate human essence of sexual attraction, one that is either directed at men or one that is directed towards women, and in which sexuality *per se* must be manifested in one of these forms. The idea here is that *sans* sexual expression and performance, one is not fully human. Undeterred by the numerous counter-examples that even contemporary societies evince; sexual essentialism denies the significance of love over sexuality, something that Sartre was insistent on. What is at issue in this form of essentialism in a two-fold position in that introduces the essentialized and static categories of man and women, and on the other it maintains that sexual preference is an essence that is established at birth. Clearly on this topic we are considering a debate of fairly long standing and yet the debate itself has all the markings of an ideological one. Sartre dealt with the issue throughout his works but more than anything else it is his debate with Freudian psychoanalysis that comprises the essence of his account. So more is at stake in the critique he offers of psychoanalysis and the core idea of repression than merely a criticism of Freud and his followers. It is really all about the use of psychology to establish a prior essence before human freedom.

Still another expression of the harmful effects of essentialist thought can be discerned in the extensions of research on adolescents and their brains, in which the so-called undeveloped teenage brain is cited as a cause for teen-age bad judgment. The argument here, an extrapolation from research in developmental psychology, is once again to remove agency from the equation of politics. However, it is often not individual agency that is being suppressed or obfuscated but the social agency implied by political obligation. It is so convenient to say, "well it was there all along, the reason why adolescents do such self-destructive things is that they don't have fully-developed brains; therefore, other than discipline not much can be done." It is interesting to consider what is lost sight of by the invocation and over-extended politicizing of this research. For example, it ignores the importance of individual and social praxis as a means whereby skills, abilities and faculties are developed. So it has little to do with the lack or realistic opportunities for learning through meaningful work that is responsible for this lack of development, no instead it is the victim's fault, in this case their underdeveloped brains.

Still another position is the argument that gender is not an ahistorical category or even one that is a permanent feature of human nature but that it is nevertheless an essential part of one's self. One can affirm being a father or a mother as an essence for them, with all of the values and so forth that go along with it. However, the difficulty here is that then such an identity comes to suspiciously resemble a role with all that that implies.

It may even be the case, as it has been with modern feminism's debate over sameness and difference, that an actual depiction of the human condition on this issue is forsworn because of the political context in which it is raised, especially since so much is at stake. There is a great deal to suggest that in fact this is the case especially when viewed as the continuation of the so-called culture wars in America. However, Sartre would have us merely consider the following observation, no matter what side of this debate one comes down on isn't it the case that in every instance it is the human being's capacity to establish a relationship that is decisive and somehow primary? For, stripped of all else that is what Sartre is saying when he describes the for-itself in its many movements, that it is a being in search of relationships and that establishing them, including ones that are negations, is what defines us. One can summarize Sartre's approach on this by recalling as scholars of phenomenology generally have, that it is simply not possible to posit a social structure of human existence, in this case that of sexuality, as an *a priori* aspect of being-with-others without, in the case of Sartre, first establishing how it is that we encounter others. Beyond that, Sartre is also deeply suspicious of the privileging of sexuality over the emotions including basic ones such as love and hate.

On this topic it will be recalled that Sartre's approach proceeds from the perspective of consciousness as opposed to subjectivity. Because the vantage point of Sartre's phenomenology is prior to subjectivity and because male and female are expressions of subjectivity, one could say there is a prior reality, one that is deeper than that of sexual preferences. This approach is particularly well suited to the study of the linkages between the human psyche and the socio-political order while at the same time providing a theory of how it is that political psychology is historically rooted. This is a major undertaking for any philosophy, still more so for one that does not approach the topic systematically, which is, of course, the case with Sartre's phenomenology. Our guide for the exposition that follows will be Sartre's interpretation of the doctrine of intentionality, the core concept of phenomenology. We will follow the priorities implied by the concept of intentionality as Sartre did and that means that we will begin our analysis with a study of the relationship between epistemology and ontology. From this vantage point we will explicate Sartre's concept of Realism as a way to formulate, from below, a view of the human condition that exposes just where essentialist claims miss the mark and just how central the intentional freedom of consciousness truly is. Next we will introduce Sartre's major social concepts, or the ones he used to delineate his social theory, the concepts of bad faith and being-with-others or *Mit-sein*. The new millennium has brought with it a dizzying array of theoretical mistakes, outright falsifications, errors and polemical overreaching and in this context a political reading of Sartre's philosophy should help clear away some debris so that politics can be seen clearly for what it is.

NOTES

1. Bernard Levy, Sartre (Cambridge, UK: Polity, 2003), 196-197.
2. Most scholars are persuaded that if one had to choose a figure from the past that exerted a strong influence of Sartre that it would be Hegel. His influence was specifically cited by Sartre. Hegel's terminology supports this view as does the existentialism implied by the theme of the "unhappy consciousness" from the *Phenomenology of Spirit*. In fact, if one preferred a second figure that influenced Sartre it would probably be Fichte whose concept of the self-positing subject is often overlooked in this regard. The author is indebted to Jay Bernstein for this insight. See especially Fichte's Theory of Subjectivity, (London: Cambridge University Press, 1990).

3. Andrew Leak, *Sartre* (London: Reaktion Books Ltd, 2006).

4. One irony here is that the author of a major work on Sartre, Bernard Henri Levy appeared on American T.V. to lambaste French students who were protesting what they viewed as a punitive labor law. Levy followed up his diatribe against the students with a call to Neoliberalism. So it's little wonder that his work reflected so little of Sartre's actual contribution to political philosophy and so much of the trivia surrounding his life and times.

5. One illustration of this trend is when the former chief of General Electric decided to write a book on his celebrated management strategies. Most reporters uniformly neglected to ask him about the wholesale pollution of the Hudson River by a General Electric plant. Instead, the former head of General Electric was greeted as an oracle.

6. One interesting but overlooked point in this regard concerns the theological implications of Sartre's concept of intentionality. The reasons it has been overlooked are by now fairly well known. For example, Sartre has for many years been considered anathema by theologians of every faith because of his explicit critique of religion and his atheism but a good deal of it traces to his denial of human nature which seems at first glace to contradict basic theological positions. However, if one really takes Sartre seriously on the priority of intentionality and the priority of consciousness over the subject, it appears that the first principle of Sartre's philosophy, from a theological point of view, is the intentional focus of human consciousness, which is of course, very close to the doctrine of intentionality in Saint Augustine. Obviously a great deal would hinge on just how one defines "nature" in this sense, as an essence of the subject or, in the case of Sartre, a feature of the ontology of being-in-the-world which Sartre, like Heidegger, considered prior to human subjectivity.

7. Specifically, Feyerabend had argued that the existential side of scientific *praxis* is both the driving force for innovation, as well as the operative epistemology. This latter epistemology has indeed come into conflict with ideological expression of science, with the end result that scientific *praxis* has been cut off from the hegemony that scientific ideologies and practices had exercised and enjoyed.

8. Sartre's critique of ideology in his later works, including ideological account of the relationship between alleged human essences and history is that when human subjectivity is placed in a more complete historical context, one that takes full account of how values, such as performance for example, support existing social and political structures, the ideological character of repressive ideologies are revealed as such.

9. Tong introduces Sartre's analysis of the emotions without seeing the truly radical point that Sartre is making about the emotions, that they provide us with a pre-cognitive understanding of the world, and, ultimately an additional basis from which to critique power structures, including those that are thoroughly sexist. Instead, like many of Sartre's critics, Tong introduces categories from the pre-cognitive level and presents them as conscious activities and choices in the social world.

10. Blanchard, R. and others, "Interaction of fraternal brother order and handedness in the development of male homosexuality," Hormone Behavior, 2006, <http://www .Ncbi.Nih.gov/entrez/query.fcgi?DB=pubmed&cmd=retrieve&list_uids=16246335& itoll=pubmed_citations&dopt=abstractplus&dr=abstractplus>. (March; 49 (3), 405-14. Epub, 2005). (2 July, 2006).

Chapter Two

Intentionality

If pressed, one would have to say that the most basic idea that Sartre is advancing, or the idea around which all of his evidence and logic is gathered, is the idea that a good, man's ability to establish relationships, is also the ability that creates the most havoc. This can be seen in the problem of reification noted in the Introduction where one first posits a relationship to something and then comes over time to perceive it as having power over one. Upon reflection it seems that this idea is a very ancient one as we see in the initial book of the Old Testament, *The Book of Genesis* where humanity is defined as the being that names things and thereby has a relationship to them.

The way that Sartre establishes his argument of course is wholly modern as is the emphasis that he places on consciousness. In terms of these relationships they are established on the basis of a *lack* or nothingness, a term that gives my friends in the analytical tradition fits. However what Sartre is actually saying is that human beings are not things even though they can establish relationships to them and make various mistakes concerning them and that we should focus not entirely on the things themselves but on the capacity that consciousness has for establishing them in the first instance. Here again though, the idea of nothingness is also of great antiquity but what distinguishes what Sartre is saying about this state from these other ancient writers especially in the Eastern tradition, is that the void that exists between consciousness and what it is conscious of is itself a motivation for both the life of the mind and social life.

So our first area of focus therefore will be to fully explicate Sartre's doctrine of Intentionality as it is related to the idea of nothingness. Here, we want to examine Sartre's position that the content of intentional consciousness *per se* is exhausted by what it is conscious of. A consideration of this will entail the importance of the idea of *nothingness* within the doctrine of Intentionality.

Our second objective will be a related one. It will involve an explication of Sartre's concept of realism, and the relationship this concept of Realism has to the emphasis that Sartre places on human agency and freedom. It is the purpose of this part of our study will be to delineate the scope of each and to explicate the consequences of each both externally as individual components of human existence and immanently as a totality that comprises the doctrine of Intentionality. Our procedure for doing so will be as follows. We will begin with the concept of "nothing." Sartre introduces this in his early work on Husserl's doctrine of Intentionality, but since that work is so brief, we will explicate it through the examples that he provides in his later works. For example, we will to analyze the concept of "nothing" in his longer study, *The Transcendence of the Ego*. Finally, we will consider the mature argument on this topic that is advanced in *Being and Nothingness*. This approach will also serve as our general guide for the analysis of the doctrine of Intentionality as a totality. However, it is important to note that *Being and Nothingness* occupies the most significant position in terms of Sartre's Doctrine of Intentionality, if not his phenomenology.

The first step in our inquiry involves an initial definition of Intentionality in Sartre's philosophy. For Sartre, Intentionality refers to a bifurcated relationship between the world and consciousness in which, from the side of the world, one encounters it on the basis of ideational action in the form of attention and constitution (an element of the convocation of intentional moments) and, from the side of consciousness, in the form of the negation of its self as an essence.

"NOTHINGNESS" IN THE ARTICLE ON INTENTIONALITY

In his earliest work on Intentionality, Sartre locates his theory in the context of Husserl's contribution to the topic: "Intentionality: A Fundamental Idea of Husserl's Phenomenology." It is a delineation of what Sartre viewed as the core idea of Phenomenology, that of the Intentionality of consciousness. Nevertheless, even though it highlights Husserl's contribution, the work contains early indications of a critique of Husserl on the basis of this core idea. For example, in this article Sartre already views Intentionality as an idea that implies a phenomenological nuance between the subject and its object. He writes that: "Consciousness has no *inside*; it is nothing but the outside of itself and it is this absolute flight, this refusal to be substance, which constitutes it as a consciousness."[1]

Consciousness is not entitative and, in fact, its state of consciousness is by definition other than what it is conscious of. It follows, therefore, that if consciousness is "other" in the way Sartre just described it, the one word that he can used to describe it is "nothing." In the encounter with objects, one is conscious of the object. But the very act of being conscious of an object implies that this encounter is defined by pure awareness and has no entitative content of its own. By positing the idea that "consciousness is nothing but the outside of itself," as he does in the article, Sartre is arguing that there is a direct relationship between consciousness and whatever it happens to be conscious *of*. This is often referred to as Sartre's "direct realism." This formulation, in which consciousness has the status of "nothing," and that this "nothingness" or lack is thereby the basis of the relationship of consciousness to the world, represents a departure from the usual conception of direct realism. Furthermore, if consciousness is truly "nothing" but the "outside of itself," then another way of formulating this is to say that awareness is purely relational. In order to give full weight to the consequences of Sartre's depiction of consciousness as "nothing," it must be that the practical meaning of the statement that consciousness is "nothing" is that it is nothing other than its relationship to the world.

In his article on Intentionality, Sartre places considerable emphasis on the importance of position in his approach. He notes: "You see this tree, all right. But you see it in the very spot where it is: on the side of the road, in the midst of the dust, alone and twisted under the heat of the sun, twenty miles away from the Mediterranean coast. There is no way it can enter your consciousness, for its nature is not that of consciousness."[2] The *epoche*, an essential element of which involves the bracketing of the "natural perspective" is part and parcel of Sartre's critique of Husserl's phenomenology and reflects a more general tension between the two philosophies regarding the priority, in the case of Sartre, of that which is "immediate." More on this will be said shortly. However, here we want to note that in his early essay on Intentionality, Sartre focuses on the direct access one has of objects as well as the fact that, for Sartre, phenomenology in effect, provides a philosophical account of immediate reality in which, as he puts it in his article: "We loathe things because they are loathsome, and love people because they are lovable."[3] The directness of being-in-the-world and amidst things was, for Sartre, the *crux* of phenomenology. On this score, it is worth noting here that Moreland, in his analysis of this question, namely that of the nature of relationship between consciousness and the world, also underscores the importance of position. For example, he notes the various possibilities open to the phenomenologist and discusses the one chosen by Sartre: "The second possibility, chosen by Sartre, is to posit a pre-reflective, non positional awareness of consciousness. In that, according to Sartre, every act of consciousness is positional; this non-positional, pre-reflective act is somehow carried along with or conjoined with every positional act of consciousness. Thus, for Sartre, consciousness is bifurcated in such a way that the relationship of consciousness to the world is grounded in a "lack," as he puts it in *Being and Nothingness*, in this particular instance, a "lack" of position. This lack of position hurls the self into the world, making it dependent on the world for its place in it. The point of origin for Sartre's realism is this radical lack of position, the emptiness of intentional consciousness (its opacity, as he puts it in *Transcendence of the Ego*), and its radical dependence.

It is also the "lack" of position and the "flight" into the world that establishes Sartre's concept of agency. The very first aspect of consciousness as bifurcated that one is introduced to in Sartre's account of Intentionality is the original negation that expels the *for-itself* into the world, thereby negating itself as substance. So, nothingness is the basis of agency in which negating is a fundamental element of human existence. Intentionality, precisely because it is the relationship between consciousness and the world, is based on nothingness. In other words, prior to the Intentionality of the intending *subject*, there exists, on Sartre's account, a prior consciousness which is itself the necessary condition for a consciousness that intends itself as reflective. That is to say, nothingness is the condition of the pre-reflective *cogito* and, in order for it to establish itself as reflective, it first must negate itself through an act of agency as being non-reflective. One can think of human agency as inextricably intertwined with the pre-reflective *cogito* since the "flight" into the world and the subsequent reflective consciousness imply agency, which, for Sartre, is established in the initial condition of "lack" or nothingness. Again, for Sartre, agency and reflection are modes of describing a fundamental relationship between consciousness and the world. Another way of formulating this, of course, is to say that the relationship between agency and Intentionality is established as part of the flight of consciousness from its capacity to render itself entitative or thing-like. On this topic, Sartre notes in his later work, *Being and Nothingness* that, "If there is to be nothingness of consciousness, there must be a consciousness which has been and which is no more and a witnessing consciousness which poses the nothingness of the first consciousness for a synthesis of recognition."[4]

The example that Sartre uses to illustrate this is that of counting a pack of cigarettes in one's pocket. Sartre notes that the first knowledge one has of this type of knowing is based on one's relationship to the world as Intentional, that is to say, as "nothing" other than the relationship. In fact, "I have a non-thetic consciousness of my adding activity. If anyone questioned me, indeed, if anyone should ask, 'What are you doing there?' I should reply at once, 'I am counting.' This reply aims not only at the instantaneous consciousness which have passed without being reflected-on, those which are forever not-re-flected-on in my immediate past."[5] Furthermore, "consciousness, as given along with the world, is prior to nothingness and is derived from being."[6] However, this is not to say that consciousness is the source of nothingness. On the contrary, in an explanatory note to that statement, Sartre states his intent: "That certainly does not mean that consciousness is the foundation of its being. On the contrary . . . We wish to only to show (1) That *nothing* is the cause of consciousness. (2) That consciousness is the cause of its own way of being."[7]

We will now turn our analysis to a consideration of "nothing" in Sartre's work, *The Transcendence of the Ego*. The fuller analysis that comprises his critique of the traditional conception of the "I" will be further considered in subsequent chapters. In *The Transcendence of the Ego*, Sartre expands on his earlier position in which the un-reflected or pre-reflective *cogito*, which he also terms a non-thetic consciousness, represents a direct encounter of the objects in the world. Sartre maintains at the conclusion of his analysis that his reversal of the usual order of consciousness, in which consciousness is said to be derived from the "I," has effected "the liberation of the Transcendental Field and at the same time its purification."[8] This is, of course, another way of approaching the issue of nothingness since, as Sartre notes in the next sentence: "In a sense, it is a *nothing*, since all physical, psycho-physical, and psychic objects, all truths, all values are outside it; since my *me* has itself ceased to be any part of it. But this nothing is *all* since it is *consciousness of* all these objects."[9] This is tantamount to a restatement of the essence of the earlier noted position expounded in the article on Intentionality. However, in this larger work, Sartre places greater emphasis on the psychology that can be derived from this concept of "nothing." For example, in order to illustrate this, he uses the example of two men, Peter and Paul, who are speaking about Peter's love. In the traditional account of such questions, one of the two individuals has access to a subjective realm that the other might try to reach, but which nevertheless remains over the horizon, and for whom the attempt to reach such a subjective realm is, "in vain."[10] For Sartre, both men have access to and speak about "the same thing." [11] Furthermore, for both men, the emotional state belongs to the transcendental field of objects, and, as such, "can be called into question."[12] Because consciousness is nothing but a revealing intuition, it has direct access to objects and states during its encounters with them. It is on that account also important to note that the interpretation of the transcendental field by way of nothingness establishes that the "I," or the subject, is not behind consciousness. One consequence of this is that for Sartre, this also means that "my emotions and my states, my ego itself, cease to be my exclusive property."[13]

In terms of the argument presented in *Transcendence of the Ego*, nothingness is also the source of the spontaneity of consciousness. Here, Sartre again
rejects the usual psychological account in which the spontaneity of consciousness springs forth from the recesses of the ego: "The commonly accepted thesis, according to which our thoughts would gush from an impersonal unconscious and would 'personalize' themselves by becoming
conscious, seems to us a coarse and materialistic interpretation of a correct intuition" (Ibid, 98). Instead, Sartre holds the view that consciousness is impersonal, which is another way of saying that it has nothing "before it". In
fact, nothingness is the basis upon which states and emotions emerge: "Thus
each instant of our conscious life reveals to us a creation *ex nihilo*."[14]

For Sartre, the transcendental field is encountered on the basis of an impersonal spontaneity, and this, at the same time, underscores Sartre's position
that the *me*, or the subject, is a derived entity. Sartre argues that this position
implies a new approach to the field of psychology. He notes: "Thus we can
distinguish, thanks to our conception of the *me*, a sphere accessible to psychology, in which the method of external observation and the introspective
method have the same rights and can mutually assist each other, and a pure
transcendental sphere accessible to phenomenology alone."[15]

There is a difficulty that Sartre acknowledges regarding his position here.
For, if consciousness is pure spontaneity, and if it is impersonal, and if, in
short, the subject is derived from consciousness, then the status of this spontaneity is potentially unsettling. Sartre refers, for example, to this spontaneity
as "monstrous" and depicts it as a source of mental illness: "It seems to us
that this monstrous spontaneity is at the origin of numerous psychasthenic ail-
ments. Consciousness is frightened by its own spontaneity because it senses
this spontaneity as *beyond* freedom."[16] It is at this juncture that the distinction
between Sartre's existential freedom and volitional freedom is most acute. We
will discuss this further in the context of Sartre's theory of the emotions; it is
noted here because Sartrean existential freedom is prior to conceptions of
freedom which are grounded in the priority of the willing subject or the "I."
The point that needs to be underscored here, however, is that the monstrous
quality of this spontaneity is nothing less than the freedom of consciousness.
One of Sartre's main points regarding intentionality is that it informs all of
one's actions and moods. This means that even in sexuality the preconditions
that are created by intentionality have a primacy. The genesis of this aspect of
intentionality is interesting for it actually originates with Saint Augustine and
was then used by Heidegger to show that intentionality pervades the structures of human acting and willing where intentionality always presupposes
the question f the meaning of being. In fact, what Heidegger referred to as authentic projection is possible in the first instance only because of the intentional horizon of the being of beings. In Augustine the very idea of willing

collapses without intentionality for it is this aspect of the mind that prevents the dispersal of the mind into that nothingness that Heidegger describes as "*fallenness.*"

Sartre's take on this aspect of intentionality is a good deal more flamboyant, and eminently more dramatic as he uses the example of human sexuality to convey the same idea. In his account of sexuality the same *angst* and ambiguity that accompanies all of one's projects appears here as well. It sexual desire and activity, Sartre argues, the entire person, and not merely their libido is at issue. In this regard Sartre's approach departs fairly dramatically from many modern accounts where sexual identity and the activities that correspond to it are but one identity among many others. Instead, Sartre would have us think of human existence as a *gestalt,* or his preferred word, totality, and so in sexual activity one feels the same potentiality for negation, shame, joy and affection that are possible in all other actions.

To illustrate this, Sartre uses the example of a young woman who is "in terror, when her husband left her alone sitting at the window and summoning the passers-by like a prostitute. Nothing in her education, neither in her past, nor in her character could serve as an explanation of such a fear. It seems to us simply that a negligible circumstance (reading, conversation, etc.) had determined in her what one might call 'vertigo of possibility.' She found herself monstrously free, and this vertiginous freedom appeared to her *at the opportunity* for this action which she was afraid of doing. But this vertigo is comprehensible only if consciousness suddenly appeared to itself as infinitely overflowing in its possibilities, the *I* which ordinarily serves as its unity."[17] So it is not her sexuality that is the basis of her *angst* as so many standard accounts would insist, but rather the existential freedom that emerges in her sexuality. The sexual interpretation of human reality, in other words, is simply not radical enough in its assessment of exactly what is taking place in the life of the individual.

For Sartre, the argument from nothingness helps to explain more of reality than accounts that place the "I" before, or behind, consciousness. This is due in part to the fact that the "monstrous" spontaneity of consciousness, while disturbing, does nevertheless offer a coherent argument, not only for why one experiences certain types of *angst*, but also for other questions. For example, one question that might be posed is this one: Why one engages in philosophical reflection in the first instance? Sartre underscores this by noting that the most primary role of consciousness is to mask or hide from consciousness its spontaneity. It is, in fact, a spontaneity that is not only free but is so "monstrously." He argues that: "Consciousness, noting what could be called the fatality of its spontaneity, is suddenly anguished: it is this dread, absolute and without remedy, this fear of itself, which seems to us constitutive of pure consciousness, and which holds the key to the psychasthenic aliment we spoke of. If the *I* of the *I think* is the primary structure of consciousness, this dread is impossible. If, on the contrary, our point of view is adopted, not only do we have a coherent explanation of this aliment, but we have, moreover, a permanent motive for carrying out the phenomenological reduction." [18]

For Sartre, the difficulty is as follows: Why would one experience existential dread if the "I" is the point of origin for consciousness? One the other hand, however, Sartre's account establishes spontaneity as "monstrous" and truly dreadful, or potentially so.

Next, Sartre invokes the tradition from Plato onward to inquire: Why it is that philosophers would engage in this activity in the first instance? To put this idea in context, it is worth recalling that Husserl in particular has posited the idea that alongside of mundane history there is another history that of motivational history within which is located the history of philosophy. Motivational, philosophical history included phenomenology ever since its origin with Thales. However, phenomenology was only present as an implied component of motivational philosophical history. When the history of philosophy is viewed in this way, one question that arises is: Why would figures such as Plato pose the question of a distinction between mundane Reality (or what can be construed as the "natural attitude") and the phenomenological, philosophical one, as Plato does in the *Allegory of the Cave*, for example?

For Sartre, the answer to this question is found in his own depiction of the rift between consciousness and the "I" and, in particular, in the fact that nothingness, as evinced by its dreadful spontaneity, is *the* point of origin for philosophy. On this score, Sartre notes that in the traditional account "one will find none of those contradictions which, according to Plato, lead the philosopher to effect a philosophical conversion."[19]

It is true, Sartre argues, that Husserl considers certain psychological motivations that *could* lead to philosophical reflection and early instances of the phenomenological reduction. However, "these motives hardly seem sufficient."[20] In fact, for Sartre, more is attained if one reverses the order and posits what is the case for him: that nothingness or "lack" is the point of origin for reflection, including philosophical reflection. As he puts it: "On the other hand, if 'the natural attitude' appears wholly as an effort made by consciousness to escape from itself by projecting itself into the *me* and becoming absorbed there, and if this effort is never completely rewarded, and if a simple act of reflection suffices in order for conscious spontaneity to tear itself abruptly away from the *I* and be given as independent, then the (*epoche*) is no longer a miracle, an intellectual method, an erudite procedure: it is an anxiety which is imposed on us and which we cannot avoid: it is both a pure event of transcendental origin and an ever possible accident of our daily life"[21]

At the conclusion of his argument, Sartre introduces the idea that nothingness establishes an unusual vantage point from which to study ethics and politics.[22] What is noteworthy here is that while he notes the issue of nothingness as a ground for political philosophy, he does not develop it. Possibly this is because of his purpose in writing *Transcendence of the Ego:* The critique of the traditional conception of the "I." However, for this present analysis, this remark at the conclusion of *Transcendence of the Ego* is extremely pertinent, especially since it occurs in the context of his discussion of nothingness. The immediate context for the remark was his critique of Left "idealism" which causes him to reassert his position that: "The world has not created me," but rather that both are "objects for a reciprocal consciousness."[23] Sartre is unequivocal about the ground of "nothing" as it relates to consciousness: "It is quite simply a first condition and an absolute source of existence. And the relation of interdependence established by this absolute consciousness between the *me* and the World is sufficient for *me* to appear as 'endangered' before the world, for the *me* (indirectly and through the intermediary of states) to draw the whole of its content from the world. *No more is needed in the way of a philosophical foundation for an ethics and a politics which are absolutely positive.*"[24]

The emphasis that Sartre places on nothingness, especially the fact that it is primary for consciousness, can often overshadow the fact that one of the consequences of his analysis is positing of a vantage point for the study of political phenomena, including ideology.

THE ARGUMENT FROM NOTHINGNESS
IN BEING AND NOTHINGNESS.

Sartre begins his analysis of the pre-reflective cogito in *Being and Nothingness* by way of establishing a contrast between his phenomenology and that of Husserl. One key aspect of that contrast is the priority that Sartre gives to ontology over epistemology. However here we wish to focus on Sartre's concept of nothingness as it relates to the pre-reflective cogito. So, for that reason we will put aside for now the contrast with Husserl as well as the relationship of epistemology and ontology.

Sartre begins his discussion by returning to the earlier relationship he discussed between consciousness and its objects. In almost identical language to that used in the article on Intentionality he notes that a table, for example, cannot be found literally in consciousness, of course, even in the form of a representation. On the contrary, for Sartre the doctrine of Intentionality establishes the independent existence of things and that there are two vantage points on this. The first is the view from the world in which Sartre's realism establishes that consciousness rests on nothing more than the object of which it is conscious. This encounter happens in the world *at* the object and, so, it is a vantage point from the world to the body. The view from consciousness, however, also involves not merely the pre-reflective cogito but the cogito *per se*. And this is a separate vantage point. The cogito may be regarded as twofold, since it involves a single relationship to the world and a reflection upon that relationship. The pre-reflective consciousness is a non-thetic one, and, since it does not have the character of a thing, it does not take on that character when it presents an object. Sartre noted that a table is not in consciousness even as a representation and argues that "a table is *in* space, beside the window, etc."[25]

For Sartre, the starting point for analysis is the emptying of things into their rightful position, as they exist only in a specific way for consciousness: "The first procedure of a philosophy ought to be to expel things from consciousness and to reestablish its true connection with the world, to know that consciousness is a positional consciousness *of* the world. All consciousness is positional in that it transcends itself in order to reach an object, and it exhausts itself in this same positing."[26]

Consciousness, in other words, contributes nothing of the content of the object of which it is conscious. Its character is to be nothing in a relationship to a something. The question arises, however: what about consciousness as it relates to itself being conscious? The *cogito* itself? For Sartre, the first thing that needs to be established is that "there must be an immediate, non-cognitive relationship of the self to itself."[27]. In terms of the immediacy of consciousness, he defines Intentionality as being-in-the-world: "The immediate consciousness which I have of perceiving does not permit me either to judge or to will or to be ashamed. It does not *know* my perception, does not *posit* it; all that there is of intention in my actual consciousness is directed toward the outside, toward the world. In turn, this spontaneous consciousness of my perception is *constitutive* of my perceptive consciousness. In other words, every positional consciousness of an object is at the same time a non-positional consciousness of itself."[28]

The immediacy to which Sartre refers here is to be understood as a pure relationship, one side of which involves the encountered object and the other side of which is a relationship to consciousness itself under its auspices as non-positional. Sartre then considers non-thetic consciousness in its bifurcation. We can see this if we recall the earlier example of counting cigarettes. Non-thetic consciousness, as the pre-reflective cogito, is purely relational and, while it is positional, it carries with it a consciousness that is non-positional. Thus, I have the experience of knowing that there is a pack of cigarettes in my pocket, and I have the knowledge that there are really a dozen. How I could know that in precise terms from the prospective of the pre-reflective cogito is vague. I know it in a relational way in the same way in which I know, while driving a car, what I need to do in order to avoid banging the sides of the car against the wall on one side of the parking space that I am entering. If someone were to ask me how much room I had on the side of the car I would, of course, need to *reflect* on what I was just doing and perhaps do a calculation. Nevertheless, the key fact for Sartre is one doesn't know how it is that ones knows the distances when parking a car, just as, in Sartre's own example, one doesn't know just how it is that one knows that there are " roughly a dozen" cigarettes in ones pocket. Sartre uses an example from Piaget's research: "Proof of this is that children who are capable of making an addition spontaneously cannot explain subsequently how they set about it."[29]

Sartre's point is to establish that it is the "non-reflective consciousness which renders the reflection possible; there is a pre-reflective cogito which is the condition of the Cartesian *cogito*."[30] The pre-reflective cogito, therefore, establishes the primacy of consciousness over the ego as well as the existence of consciousness of the relationship to the world that is characterized by nothingness.

INTENTIONALITY AND REALISM

Sartre viewed the promise of phenomenology as residing in the fact that it offered a more credible account of the "realist" position. But what does Sartre mean by Realism? Because it is related to his doctrine of Intentionality, it is in fact, a extremely complex doctrine, that he exposits slightly differently in each of his major early works. For example, in *The Transcendence of the Ego* it may be viewed as an attempt to reestablish the Realism he originally found in Husserl's phenomenology, and, to a certain extent *Transcendence of the Ego* represents an attempt to posit this point. In fact, a contrast may be drawn between Sartre's focus on Husserl's Realism in *Transcendence of the Ego*, and his focus on the Realism involved in freedom and especially as it relates to bad faith in *Being and Nothingness*. With regard to the earlier text, our immediate focus here, it is worth noting that Sartre held that the commitment to "realism" was precisely what was called into question by Husserl's exposition of transcendental phenomenology. For, even at the outset of his later arguments against Husserl, Sartre contends that he plans to demonstrate that the ego is "neither formally nor materially *in consciousness*; (emphasis added) it is outside, in the world.[31] As McCulloch notes, Sartre's "realist" position thus does involve an "externalism." However, as this analysis will underscore, it is considerably more complex than that of merely describing a venue for consciousness that stands over and against an interior one.

Sartre contrasts his position with that of Husserl in *Ideas*, where, according to Sartre, there is a return to the classical position of a Transcendental "I," or ego: "After having determined that the me is a synthetic and transcendent production of consciousness, he reverts in *ideen Zu Einer Reinen Phanomenologie Und Phenomenologischen Philosophie* to the classic position of a transcendental 'I'. This 'I' would be, so to speak, behind each consciousness, a necessary structure of consciousness whose rays would light upon each phenomenon presenting itself in the field of attention. Thus, transcendental consciousness becomes thoroughly personal. Was this notion necessary? Is it compatible with the definition of consciousness given by Husserl?"[32]

Sartre's rejoinder to this position is that phenomenology "does not need to appeal to any such confirming and individualizing 'I.' Indeed consciousness is defined by Intentionality."[33] In other words, for Sartre it is not the mind that provides the unity of perception but rather the object itself. For, as noted earlier, the subject is expelled into the world in the first instance by a "lack." The point here is the reiteration of this aspect of phenomenology, this time from the vantage point of the self's "lack" of an "essence." Consciousness thus, is an encounter with the object, which is an intersection of consciousness and object. In other words, it is an in-between by virtue of its being-in-the-world. He notes in this regard that: "The object is transcendent to the consciousness which grasps it and it is in the object that the unity of consciousness is found."[34] Consciousness also provides, thereby, a temporal synthesis in that it is a convocation of intentional moments of encounter with objects and being-in-the-world generally.

Sartre's doctrine of Intentionality positions the *for-itself* at the intersection of subjectivity and objectivity. That is to say, as a being-in-the-world the for-itself is not only inter-subjective but it is also inter-worldly (or between subjectivity and objectivity). Furthermore, by arguing for the priority of Intentionality in this way, Sartre is also arguing against the priority of the "scientific" account of Reality, be it the "science" of the animating construal of Husserl's phenomenology, or that of historical, conditioned determinations of consciousness, such as ideology. Another way of saying this is that Sartre is arguing for *praxis* as the point of origin for understanding the world and against the priority of the "reification" of consciousness.[35] For example, Sartre's version of direct Realism posits the "reification" of consciousness as being derived from a primordial relationship to the world.

In terms of classical phenomenology, of course, for Sartre there is a bias in favor of the actual, or natural, that gives it a priority over something as it is established under the reduction. On this score, Sartre's depiction of Intentionality

seems to diverge from Husserl's on the question of the *eidetic* reduction. The
so-called "natural" perspective was for him not the truth of the notion, but
rather the starting point for an inquiry into the truth. But, as we have indicated
above, this issue is far more complex than that of a mere difference of procedure. It is true that the idea of *eidetic* reduction is absent from Sartre's phenomenology.[36] However, the issue of ontology *per se* in Husserl and Sartre
makes their relationship far more complex then merely that of differences regarding the bracketing of the natural perspective. For, insofar as Phenomenology represents the attempt to go beyond epistemology towards ontology,
it may be said that both Sartre and Husserl posit a reduction that works towards the selfsame *telos*. This relationship between Husserl and Sartre is captured in the fact that neither reduction is compatible with a de-ontological approach, for example. In the latter account, the empirical, experienced world is
the most significant and represents most real. However, for both Husserl and
Sartre, just because one has an empirical experience, it does not follow that
that experience represents a terminus. Instead, for both philosophers, there is
an ontological level that is prior as the given. We will see this a bit more directly when we consider Sartrean Realism from the perspective of the *vicious*,
in which, famously, the empirical experience of the chestnut tree in *Nausea*
belies the fact that the truly most real experience (i.e., total and primordial),
is that of the existential encounter with the reality of the chestnut tree.

There are important differences between the two thinkers. For example,
Sartre's explication and emphasis of nothingness as the basis for the phenomenological claim to being. On this score, one argument introduced by
Sartre in *Transcendence of the Ego,* is that one simply must continue the reduction to include consciousness itself. When this is undertaken, Sartre argues, the only position one can avow is that of a twofold relationship between
being and nothing in which both are coeval with and constitutive of both consciousness and world. To put the matter otherwise, the discontinuity between
the two modalities of consciousness is what establishes the world as a venue
or horizon for the consciousness of entities in the world, as well as the being
of consciousness itself—its own self-reflection. For Sartre, as it is sometimes
put, it is a matter of "this tree" that one encounters and one does so not solely
via Reason. Importantly for Sartre, this encounter can take place through the
emotions, or the imagination, as well as through Reason. The issue here is
that of the immediate relationship that informs Sartre's approach to these human faculties of mind. For, while there are numerous variations under which
Husserl's eidetic reduction are undertaken, some of which certainly involve
the use of imagination, for Sartre the emphasis is on the ontological event, or
on the encounter between the object and consciousness as *for-itself*. The immediacy of this encounter, be it the chestnut tree of *Nausea*; the Japanese

mask in the article on Intentionality, or *le regard* in *Being and Nothingness* speaks to the fact that for Sartre, "Consciousness is a being whose existence posits its essence, and inversely it is consciousness of a being, whose essence implies its existence; that is, in which appearance lays claim to being."[37]

This may be a useful juncture to elaborate further on Sartre's Realism. On this score, it is worth noting that McCulloch identifies two versions of realism that were rejected by Sartre. The first, Cartesian realism, in which *cogito ergo sum* serves as the guarantor of mathematical truths and where the dichotomy between mind and body is accentuated on that basis, was famously rejected by Sartre even as early as his work on *The Transcendence of the Ego*. The second version, metaphysical realism or, as McCulloch terms it, "sometimes Platonism," posits the "universals" as the most real, as evinced in Plato's *Allegory of the Cave*. This is also rejected by Sartre.[38] Before proceeding to further delineate Sartrean Realism it would be worthwhile to look first at a particular aspect of Realism in Sartre and Husserl. The thought that we are advancing here is that it may be useful to highlight their differences and further bring into relief the uniqueness of Sartre's doctrine of Realism.

The point that should be noted regarding realism in Husserl and Sartre involves a refinement of the question of Husserl's reduction, that of essences. In this regard, Sartre makes the following point regarding the issue of reduced essence: it is Sartre's position that the (formal) reduction ignores something of equal importance for phenomenology, the status of the immediately given itself. Here, the issue is that of the world itself as it appears under the modality of the natural attitude. The experience of the chestnut tree as "other," as "boiled leather," for example, may be depicted as a psychological state, one appearance among many that, in Husserlian terms, needs to be bracketed in the quest for the essence of the chestnut tree. However, for Sartre, the experience of the chestnut tree reveals more than its usual characteristics. The most primordial revealed essence of the chestnut tree is its existence, or its location within existential Realism. It is revealed in this manner not because of a psychological state, but because of the Intentionality of consciousness as a "lack," and as an in-between that can delineate the existence of things. The presence of both non-thetic and thetic consciousness equips one with the ability to discern existence *per se*. It shares being with other beings the being of in-itself, of course, but it is also thereby nothingness, and so it is able, as for-itself, to view being *per se*. This amounts to what appears to be a contradictory pursuit of existential essence, which is tantamount to an inquiry into the relationship between nothingness and Reality.

We can see from this that Husserl's position is problematic for Sartre since the whole point of phenomenology rests on its potential as realism, the focus of his earlier noted works on the topic. It is clear, for example, that even in his early essay on Husserl's doctrine of Intentionality, his own interpretation of Husserl departs significantly from that of Husserl on the nature of the "*eidetic* reduction." Nowhere in the essay on "Intentionality" is there a reference to the philosophy of mind that played such a pivotal role in all of Husserl's approaches to the topic. Instead, there is an overwhelming emphasis on the coordinates of the Real, or natural world, as they relate to consciousness. Also, already, in these early texts there is the outline of an ego that has been removed—replaced by a void at the very center on consciousness—a void that Sartre will later term "nothingness," or a "lack" that is the ground of being. There is, then, an explicit emphasis on the "natural world," and the "social world" as it is presented in the initial, or immediate.

In sum then, the "natural perspective," underscores the differences between Sartrean and Husserlian phenomenology, but as we saw in the discussion of essence in both thinkers, these differences are about more than the formal bracketing of the natural perspective. The core of the issue also involves the relationship between nothingness and Reality. It is this difference which ultimately informs their respective differences regarding the term, essence. A nuance here is that Husserl's method is not intended to diminish the force of Reality from the vantage point of ontology, relative to epistemology, but instead involves an attempt to grasp the "essence" of the object as ontological. Furthermore, additional complexity resides in the fact that Husserl's position involves an eventual repositioning of reduced essences ultimately in a "life world." For Husserl, this is accomplished through the *epoche* as a formal inquiry using Reason, and it represents a pivotal aspect of his interpretation of phenomenology. If we take this as our cue, then, along these lines, one could argue, that this Realism, is in fact more "real" than that of Sartre. If such a line of reasoning was employed, it would proceed to note that the natural perspective is in point of fact a reified one, and that the distillation and rigor of the reduction is tantamount to making a clear distinction between the reified world of the everyday and the actually "real" world given only through the use of the reduction. Such a position would be akin to McCulloch's depiction of Platonic realism in his analysis of this issue.[39] However, one important element of Sartre's Realism is the direct encounter *in* the world and not *within* the mind as traditionally depicted. Here we are referring to Sartre's radicalism as evinced in his idea that being-in-the-world is an in-between nothingness and consciousness, according to which consciousness itself is bifurcated.

On the topic of realism in Husserl and Sartre it may also be emphasized that for Husserl there is almost an exclusive emphasis on the role of Reason. It is the primary means for discovering what is real. The latter is disclosed primarily through the use of Reason as it attempts to derive the truth by way of the reduction. For Husserl this is evident in history. It is, therefore, in history that one finds that "motivational" or "intentional" history begins with the introduction of philosophy in the West through the philosopher Thales, and furthermore, that this introduction represents the attempt to distinguish the actually real from mundane history, the latter of which, it could be argued, is precisely the one that is "reified."[40]

The contrast with Sartre on this point is acute. For Sartre, one point of origin in terms of understanding Reality can be the emotions. The examples he uses involve absurdity, a reflection of the relationship between nothingness and Reality. Absurdity is a fact that one learns from one's own immediate, emotional experience of existence. One does not need to approach this through the use of a phenomenological reduction. Instead, it is the very structure of consciousness, including its unique bifurcated status in an environment comprised of things and others that highlights this aspect of the *really real*.

Sartre also provides a kind of "argument from music" and one can use it to illustrate this point. Sartre uses music to underscore his version of direct realism. As we saw earlier in the depiction from *Nausea*, the experience of the being of beings is horrifying. However, this is not only because it is ambiguous, or as we will soon term it, *viscous*, but because it is amorphous. It overflows everything as it posits one's states of consciousness as grounded in a "lack" or nothingness. By way of introduction, one may want to ask: When faced with a similar theoretical challenge, how to depict authenticity in a context that is defined by "fallenness" (a type of alienation), Heidegger developed the argument from "projection." But what about Sartre?

Although it initially appears to be the case that Sartre follows Heidegger on this, having his character in *Nausea* effect a reversal in his life's plan in which he gives up his research on the "grand bourgeois" for something more authentic and personal, in fact for Sartre the position of consciousness is more delicate than that of Heidegger's *Dasein*. On this score, it is important to note that at important junctures in *Nausea,* Sartre uses the occasion of musical arrangement, in particular the song, "Some of these Days" to suggest that musical arrangement "totalizes" (to use a term of Sartre's later works) the amorphous quality of existence and renders it comprehensible. The sequence of musical notes has the effect of rendering the encounter with existence itself as structured and personal. It is a personal and immediate experience of time in that it amounts to Intentionality unifying itself in its convocation of the moments of temporality. The view that is advanced is that this takes place because the stream of consciousness replaces the amorphous encounter with one that is personal and social, both non-thetic and thetic. If we return again to *Nausea*, and to the description of a chestnut tree, we see that Sartre illustrates his argument through depictions of the imagination and the emotions. For, what is noteworthy in this description is not only that Sartre's account involves an emotion, but that this emotion is coeval with an actual object, in this instance a natural object. The delineation of both poles of existence, to use Husserlian terminology, involves not only objectivity, as McCulloch and others rightly note, but it also involves something else: a rather complex emotional theory that will be considered separately when this analysis considers Intentionality from the perspective of Sartre's existential psychoanalysis. We will see that his perspective is both a critique of traditional psychoanalysis as well as a competing psychological and anthropological version of realism. In short, for Sartre, the emotions represent an additional language or media for assessing the immediately given. This is not to say that Reason is diminished, but only that the Imagination, and, as we will see, the emotions, are also revelatory of existential Reality. Here, it may be useful to cite the actual scene in *Nausea* where Sartre's character Antoine Roquentin encounters, what is for Sartre, the true essence of the chestnut tree:

> "So I was in the park just now. The roots of the chestnut tree were sunk in the ground just under my bench. I couldn't remember it was a root any more . . . I was sitting, stooping forward, head bowed, alone in front of this black, knotty mass, entirely beastly, which frightened me. Then I had this vision . . . I was like the others . . . I said, like them, 'the ocean is green; that white speck up there is a seagull,' but I didn't feel that it existed or that the seagull was an 'existing seagull'; usually existence hides itself . . . And then all of a sudden, there it was, clear as day: existence had suddenly unveiled itself. It had lost the harmless look of an abstract category: it was the very paste of things, this root was kneaded into existence . . . The chestnut tree pressed itself against my eyes. Green rust covered it half-way up; the bark, black and swollen, looked like boiled leather."[41]

Sartre depicts this experience of Reality as an encounter with being *per se*. The experience is characterized as amorphous, ambiguous, and, in a word, viscous. Again, we will discuss Sartre's argument from the viscous shortly. However, here we wish merely to underscore a fundamental feature of Sartre's Realism. It is an encounter with being that may be discerned by the emotions, the imagination, or Reason. For Sartre, the encounter can initially involve the pre-reflective *cogito*, and often only later on is it grasped by one's reasoning faculties. The paradigmatic text for this, of course, is *Nausea*. But it is also presented formally by Sartre in his philosophical works, *Transcendence of the Ego* and *Being and Nothingness*. Furthermore, one can view this as a developmental variation on Husserl's reduction with the important caveats that have already been introduced: that of the coeval status of the emotions and the faculty of imagination in Sartre, as well as the structure of consciousness as non-thetic and as thetic. Parenthetically, it can be noted that in terms of methodology, the distinction between Sartre and Husserl on this is quite striking. For, leaving aside the imagery and hyperbole, there are considerable distinctions between the Husserlian example of a reduced object in *Ideas I* and Sartre's depiction of the reduction of the chestnut tree just recounted from the pages of *Nausea*.

Before concluding this chapter we should address an objection concerning Sartre's realism. We should begin by discussing the fact that there is indeed an "existential *epoche*" that operates in Sartre's phenomenology, and it is such that it may be described as a bracketing of the natural attitude in order to highlight the existentially real. This can be made clearer perhaps if we consider an objection that may be raised concerning Sartre's approach. It could, for example, be objected that Sartre's direct Realism is unintelligible without positing what is generally accepted about the encounter with the "Other." It may be recalled that in the article on "Intentionality," Sartre had maintained that when we love someone it is because he or she really is lovable. However, it also seems irrefutable that psychological factors play an important role regarding who is lovable and who is not. The answer that Sartre provides to this in *Being and Nothingness* is that of a significantly expanded account of *Mitsein*. But what about the earlier works? What answer can be derived from these accounts which seem to emphasize Sartre's direct realism in its most radical form? It seems to us that one can answer this objection to Sartre's direct realism by looking at the issue from a category of Sartre's phenomenology that is often subsumed within the doctrine of Intentionality itself: the fact that Sartre's phenomenology is, at its core, a relational phenomenology. That is to say, because non-thetic consciousness is already encountering objects (and thereby consciousness is grounded on that relationship) it is not only a relationship between the Intending consciousness and the object or other, but is also a relationship between consciousness and reflected consciousness. It is, in short, a component of one's own ontology, that of the bifurcated relationship between consciousness as in-itself and for-itself. Generally speaking, this point is made in a different context, as noted above, in the more mature work, *Being and Nothingness*, where the Other is a mediation of "recognition." So, on the one hand, consciousness has a direct relationship to what it encounters, but also, on the other hand, it has a thetic relationship that is layered by the experiences that it has such that its field is textured by moments of Intentionality. Sartre's rejection of the traditional "I" means that in order for him to fully explicate a phenomenological account of Reality, there must be some other operation by which conditioned responses, no matter how seemingly immediate, or seemingly innate, are to be accounted for. For Sartre, it is the effect of layering within the transversals of Intentionality, itself the result of a more fundamental relationship between consciousness and the world.[42] We can put this in terms of the distinctions we have been making here between Husserl and Sartre where an important nuance concerns the *epoche* in Sartre and Husserl. For Sartre, what is involved is the horizon of Intentionality. Husserl, on the other hand uses the reduction in order to, at the end of the day, reestablish the real in a new, more accurate light, but one that is thoroughly informed by Reason.

NOTES

1. Jean-Paul Sartre, Intentionality, a Fundamental Idea of Husserl's Phenomenology," trans. Joseph P. Fell *British Journal of Phenomenology*, 1, (1970): 1-5
2. Ibid.: 4-5.
3. Ibid.
4. Jean-Paul Sartre, Being and Nothingness (New York: Washington Sq. Press, 1966): lxvi.
5. Ibid: lxiii.
6. Ibid: lxvi.
7. Ibid: n.5.
8. Jean-Paul Sartre (New York: Farrar, Straus and Giroux, 1991): 93.
9. Ibid.
10. Ibid.: 95
11. Ibid.
12. Ibid.
13. Ibid.: 94.
14. Ibid.: 98-99
15. Ibid.: 96.
16. Ibid,: 99.
17. Ibid.: 100.
18. Ibid.
19. Ibid.:102.
20. Ibid.
21. Ibid.:103.
22. Here, of course, Sartre is referring to the *epoche* as evinced in philosophical inquiry *per se,* and not the more technical distinction between Husserl and himself on the philosophical question of Realism.
23. Ibid.: 106.
24. Ibid.
25. Sartre, op.cit., 1966: lxi.
26. Ibid.: lxi.
27. Ibid.: lxii
28. Ibid.: lxii-lxiii.
29. Ibid.: lxii.

30. Ibid.: lxii.

31. Sartre, *Transcendence of the Ego* (New York: Farrar, Straus and Giroux, 1991): 31.

32. Ibid.: 37.

33. Ibid.: 38.

34. Ibid.

35. This difference surfaces in a number of Sartre's works, but perhaps nowhere more significantly than in Sartre's introduction to the *Critique of Dialectical Reason* in which he argues the case for a *praxis* that develops out of "scarcity" in such a way that it ushers in a choice between *praxis* and negation. This view will be contrasted with Marcuse's account of reification, and the phenomenon of "repression."

36. It is true that one can speak of a "reduction" in Sartre with respect to a terminus in human agency or freedom, and in this context one can examine works such as *Anti-Semite and Jew,* or Sartre's analysis of bad faith and make a case for the presence of a "reduction" that is operative in Sartre's phenomenology.

37. Sartre, op. cit.,1966: lxxiv.

38. Gregory McCulloch, *Using Sartre* (London: Routledge, 1994): 118.

39. Husserl also discusses this form of "realism" in Book One of Ideas. In section 22, he considers Platonic 'realism' from a critical the perspective: "The Reproach of Platonic Realism. Essence and Content" Edmund Husserl, *Ideas* tr. Kersten (Hague: Nijhoff,1983): 40-43.

40. Thus, for one group of philosophers in the tradition of Plato, Aristotle, Hegel and Marx, the immediate is 'reified' and Reason only can discern the "real." For another group consisting of Heraclitus, Hobbes, Heidegger and Sartre, the immediately given is true, and ideology, if not reification, is introduced through the use of a type of reasoning.

41. Jean-Paul Sarte, *Nausea* (New York: New Directions, 1964): 170–172.

42. Calvin O. Schrag, *The Self After Postmodernity* (New Haven: Yale, 1999).

Chapter Three

The Debate with Husserl: on the Subject

In this part of our analysis, we will continue our study of Sartre's Realism with particular attention to the relationship between Intentionality and Realism. As noted in the Introduction, this is not merely a philosophical concern but a political one as well because the issue of human nature remains a pivotal category for political theory *per se* in that one's position on questions of human nature informs the kinds of politics and policies that one is likely to subscribe to. So it is by the same fact a pivotal category for political ideology as well.

Specifically, the question that will guide this section of our analysis is the question of just how it is possible to give an account of direct realism while rejecting the traditional formula regarding consciousness. Once again, that perspective, unlike the one advanced by Sartre, is that the ego gives rise to consciousness. On this score, one might want to know, for example, how it is that the ego is not at the very least a filter for encounters in the world.

It is important to recall that for Sartre the world that is given in the way phenomenology depicts it includes the social world. The latter may also be described as an intersubjective one, but, interestingly, the consensus view on Sartre's account is that it was only in his middle period, especially that of *Being and Nothingness*, that the emphasis on intersubjectivity is given an emphasis. This may be supported by the numerous critiques of Sartre's early work, which in the main focus on what is often referred to as his excessive individualism. Along these lines, this view contends, it is only with *Being and Nothingness* that the emphasis on *Mit-sein* appears, and it is this concept, more than any other, that allows Sartre to finally put to rest the charges of solipsism. This view is largely correct, but only to a point, and so we will begin our analysis here by citing examples of Sartre's early works that seem to underscore and support de Beauvoir's defense of Sartre's early works in which de Beauvoir discerns a strong current of inter-subjectivity. The view that is advanced here, and that has been annunciated earlier, is that this defense is partial, and that a stronger defense lies in the combination of Realism and Intentionality that is part and parcel of Sartre's earliest contributions. Such a focus has the effect of highlighting both inter-worldness and intersubjectivity.

For Sartre, the social component of being-in-the-world, such as the waiter and the relationship between his identity and his actions, is underscored in *Being and Nothingness*. Its fullest delineation is put forth in *The Critique of Dialectical Reason*, where being-in-the-world represents a being that is "situated" and which is itself a necessary condition for the *group-in-fusion*, or even for *praxis* (as opposed to *alterity*). Yet, even in the early article on phenomenology, one can see the importance of the "situation" for the individual. For example, he opens his article on Intentionality with a quasi-sexual reference or allusion. He then introduces his main point and that is that consciousness and the world are given at once. However, if Intentionality is not grounded in the transcendental "I," then how does Sartre establish the continuity of consciousness? The answer is that for Sartre the subject as an ego has been replaced by consciousness, a state of affairs wherein consciousness is nothing but "a strong wind" or a transparency. So, the question becomes more pressing. On this score, Sartre even goes further and maintains: "If by an impossible chance, you were to enter 'into' a consciousness, you would be seized by a whirlwind and thrown back outside, near the tree, in the midst of the dust, for consciousness has no 'inside'; it is nothing but the outside of itself and it is this absolute flight, this refusal to be substance which constitute it as a consciousness."[1]

This same question, when viewed from an epistemological point of view, may be reformulated: If it is not the transcendental "I," or the "I" of the Tradition, or indeed any expression of the ego that provides the basis for knowledge of the distinction between the "real world" and the seemingly real, then what does?

The key to Sartre's reply is the idea that: "Consciousness and world are given in one shot."[2] For Sartre this statement involves making a choice between the traditional ground of epistemology (the "I"), and the claims of radical freedom. Given absolute freedom, Sartre asks, what must be true concerning the ground of epistemology? It is a theme that Sartre returns to again and again in the course of his philosophical explications. For example, in *Being and Nothingness*, he notes: "We deliberately begin with the abstract if we question experience as Kant does, inquiring into the conditions of its possibility—or if we effect a phenomenological reduction like Husserl, who would reduce the world to the state of the noema-correlate of consciousness."[3]

Instead, Sartre reverses the order. It is not the "I" that synthetically unifies consciousness, but rather it is consciousness, which has the ontological status of *nothing*, that creates the "I." As he puts it at the conclusion of *The Transcendence of the Ego*: "The Transcendental Field, purified of all ego-logical structure, recovers its primary transparency. In a sense, it is a *nothing*, since all physical, psycho-physical and psychic objects, all truths, all values are outside it. . . ."[4] One might ask, of course, how this is possible, and Sartre provides the following analysis of his view regarding the cause of the illusion of the ego: "The ego is an object apprehended, but it is also an object *constituted*, by reflective consciousness, and its products—internalized features of the socialization process. The ego is a virtual locus of unity, and consciousness constitutes it in a direction contrary to that actually taken by the production: really, consciousnesses are first; these are constituted states; and then, through the latter, the ego is constituted. But as the order is reversed by a consciousness which imprisons itself in the world in order to flee from itself, consciousnesses are given as emanating from states, and states as produced by the ego. It follows that consciousness projects its own spontaneity into the ego-object in order to confer on the ego the creative power absolutely necessary to it."[5]

Sartre puts the matter this way in *Being and Nothingness*: "If someone asks what this *nothing* is which provides a foundation for freedom, we shall reply that we cannot describe it since it *is not*, but we can at least hint at its meaning by saying that this nothing is made-to-be by the human being in his relation with himself."[6] Sartre touches on this again toward the conclusion of *Being and Nothingness* where he is looking back on the role of *nothing* in the structure of consciousness and its significance for freedom: "Thus freedom is a lack of being in relation to a given being; it is not the upsurge of a full being. And if it is this hole of being, this nothingness of being as we have just said, it supposes all being in order to rise up in the heart of being as a hole."[7] In terms of his critique of Husserl, Sartre is quite blunt: "The phenomenological conception of consciousness renders the unifying and individualizing role of the 'I' totally useless. It is consciousness, on the contrary, which makes possible the unity and the personality of my 'I', the transcendental 'I', therefore, has no *raison d' etre*."[8]

It is interesting that Sartre attributes to Husserl this depiction of a law of existence even while distancing himself from Husserl's interpretation of that law. "Indeed the existence of consciousness is an absolute because consciousness is consciousness of itself. That is to say, the type of existence of consciousness is to be consciousness of itself. And consciousness is aware of itself in so far as it is consciousness of a transcendent object. All is therefore clear and lucid in consciousness: the object with its characteristic opacity is before consciousness, but consciousness is purely and simply consciousness of being consciousness of that object. This is the law of existence."[9]

Before proceeding, it is also important to note how, for Sartre, the ego arises as a reflective creation of past acts of consciousness. On this score there are a few points that should be noted. In the first instance, being-in-the-world is intentional, which, as Sartre argues in the "Ontological Proof" means that consciousness is born supported by a "lack," it is not entitative as are the things that it encounters. Secondly, intentionality is a stream: "We must further understand that the intentions aim at appearances which are never to be given at one time. It is an impossibility on principle for the terms of an infinite series to exist all at the same time before consciousness. . . ."[10] Finally, being-in-the-world is relational for Sartre, which means that with regard to temporality, it is establishment or positing of itself as appearance. The latter represents the basis for his depiction of "bad faith," a topic that will be addressed shortly and which is mentioned here because it involves mistaking immanence for transcendence and transcendence for immanence. It is also expressed when the idea of a timeless ego is depicted as giving rise to temporality, rather than what is the case for Sartre: that the intentionality of consciousness gives rise to the temporality of the ego. Sartre makes this point succulently in his analysis of the future in his section on "Temporality" in *Being and Nothingness*: "Only a being which has to be its being instead of simply being it can have a future."[11] The upshot of temporality for Sartre is that the human experience of time in the manner of past, present and future is discernable only on the basis of a fundamental state of being-in-the-world, and this evinces a basic temporality that corresponds to it. As he puts it: "The only possible method by which to study temporality is to approach it as a totality which dominates its secondary structures and which confers on them their meaning."[12] It is this basic state of being-in-the-world, of course, that constitutes the full measure of Sartre's Realism. It is from this that the essence of Sartre's position on the self follows. Indeed, the remaining focus of his analysis in the *Transcendence of the Ego* consists in explicating this position. It is an argument that Sartre supports with examples taken from everyday, social life. For example, Sartre contends that the operational meaning of the idea that consciousness is always consciousness of something is the correlative whereby the object of which consciousness is aware is the foundation of consciousness itself.

In this view, freedom surfaces as being directly related to the Reality behind the argument. One interesting and important aspect of Sartre's realism is its relationship to freedom, and it may be stated as follows: Because consciousness rests on nothing other than what it is conscious of (a Sartrean Reality principle) one is existentially free, or intentionally so, relative to objects,

Others, and states. It is, in short. an immanent theory of liberation. It is in this sense that freedom for Sartre is a universal mandate. In *The Transcendence of the Ego,* one encounters Sartre's unique depiction of freedom as a phenomenon that is coeval with the intentionality of consciousness, this much is well established. However, it is also a text that suggests a relationship between world freedom and the freedom of consciousness or its Intentionality. On that account, it represents a departure from the "Tradition," since it is not primarily an elaboration of the freedom of the individual as an expression of the human capacity to make moral decisions as much as it is a condition of being human. Again, this position is also closely tied to the phenomenology of consciousness, since it is the latter that provides the unity of consciousness. The "Tradition," in Sartre's view, had erroneously given this phenomenological condition the term "I." It is erroneous in Sartre's view because: "the Transcendental 'I' is nothing but the death of consciousness."[13] For Sartre, this is because the very structure of the *in-itself* and the *for-itself* requires that consciousness must not be an entity as the *in-itself* is. Instead, it must remain relational. Indeed, it is on the basis of the relationship between the for-itself and the in-itself that Sartre will make his case that freedom is the only absolute — the practical meaning for Sartre of the statement that consciousness and world are given as one.[14] We may restate this as suggesting that the fate of one as a free agent is tied to that of the Other.

FURTHER DISTINCTIONS BETWEEN HUSSERL AND SARTRE

We will now sharpen some aspects of Sartre's departure from the traditional account of the ego by comparing Sartre's version of the Intentionality of consciousness with that of Husserl. Our purpose in doing so is to continue our exposition of Sartrean realism. On this score, there are two objections to Sartre's view that will be considered in this portion of our study. The first will involve Simone de Beauvoir's defense of Sartre against the charge, most notably by Merleau-Ponty, that Sartre's phenomenology is excessively subjectivist. The second objection that will be addressed is that of Edie, who argues that Sartre's account is tantamount to a misreading of Husserl.

With regard to these points there are two issues that are extremely pertinent and that will need to be addressed as part of our study. The first is the issue of intersubjectivity. It is nothing less than the cornerstone of de Beauvoir's defense of Sartre. The second issue, and the one that corresponds to Edie's analysis. pertains to Sartre's doctrine of Intentionality itself. This is likewise an essential point. What makes Sartre's Intentionality such a radical idea is that it establishes freedom in a different and more fundamental way. It is directly tied to a depiction of Realism that is itself as radical as the concept of freedom it advances. Husserl simply did not place the emphasis on freedom in the way that Sartre did. Finally, proceeding in this fashion will enable us to begin establishing important links among other aspects of Sartre's philosophy, such as that of the relationship among freedom, Realism and bad faith upon which Sartre's critique of ideology is founded. It also serves as an important linkage between the early phenomenology of consciousness that Sartre advances and the qualified but complex role he assigns to *Mit-sein* in his middle and later works.

As noted, Sartre disputes and negates the concept and structure of the Transcendental "I." Again, his argument is that there is simply no fundamental place for it in a correctly explicated account of the Intentionality of consciousness. Furthermore, he elaborates on this point further: "But if the 'I' were a necessary structure of consciousness, this opaque 'I' would at once be raised to the rank of an absolute. We would be in the presence of a monad. And this, indeed, is unfortunately the orientation of the new thought of Husserl. Consciousness is loaded down; consciousness has lost that character which rendered it the absolute existent by virtue of *non-existence*. It is heavy and ponderable. All the results of phenomenology begin to crumble if the *I* is not, by the same title as the world, a relative existent: that is to say, an object *for* consciousness."[15] To reiterate: for Sartre, there are two choices at this juncture. Either one can make of the "I" an absolute, in which case it would be a monad—self-contained, and immutable. The other choice is to view consciousness as primary, in which case one must account for the fact of the "I," while at the same time accounting for the facticity of the world. Sartre's solution is to establish "nothingness," the situation whereby consciousness is neither entitative, since it is radically free, nor an essence, since it establishes the ego subsequent to the intentionality of consciousness—for the distinction itself whereby the structure of consciousness is both *in-itself* and *for-itself* is "nothing." Of course, the question arises: Does the position that Sartre advances—that consciousness rests on nothing more than the object of which it is conscious—foreclose any continuity of the self?

In order to fully address this question, the analysis should underscore the place of intersubjectivity in Sartre's phenomenology, for, as de Beauvoir notes, the intersubjective field implies a history, and, likewise, it also implies a continuity of individual existence as well. The introduction to intersubjectivity is the earlier noted concept of "constitution," with the proviso that for Sartre, "constitution" refers to the constitution of the subject as well as everything else.

INTERSUBJECTIVITY IN SARTRE'S
ACCOUNT OF INTENTIONALITY

The question of constitution is an important one for Husserlian scholars. However, for Sartre, the more important question is not that of the venue for constitution, but rather the question concerning the structure of the constituting consciousness itself. True, there is an implied sense in which Husserl may be said to have been concerned with this aspect of Intentionality, but at the end of the day, Husserl is generally considered to have had as his focus the establishment of science essences with all that it implies: reason as the sole vehicle for discerning essences, a reduction that is an eidetic reduction, and an interpretation of the ego that supervises the whole process. By way of contrast, for Sartre, constitution is nothing so much as a convocation of the temporality of different intentional experiences.

These experiences presuppose a social world in which one encounters Others as well as things. This is a point that was addressed, or perhaps underscored, by de Beauvoir in her defense of Sartre's philosophy against Merleau-Ponty's critique. That defense hinges on de Beauvoir's argument that Sartre's philosophy is not a solipsism, but is a philosophy in which the intersubjective field necessitates a philosophy of history—the exact area of focus in Merleau-Ponty's critique. De Beauvoir notes that Sartre's account of consciousness is not a radical subjectivity as Merleau-Ponty argues, but instead (echoing a point made earlier), it is a state of affairs in which the subject is created by consciousness: "Sartre's philosophy has never been a philosophy of the subject, and he seldom uses this word by which Merleau-Ponty indiscriminately designates consciousness, the Ego (*Moi*), and humanity. For Sartre, consciousness's pure presence to self is not a subject."[16] Of course, de Beauvoir cites passages such as the following from *Being and Nothingness* to make the point that Sartre's phenomenology involves an intersubjective field (and, by extension, is not a solipsism): "We, on the contrary, have shown that the self on principle cannot inhabit consciousness" (Ibid). But what about Sartre's early works? On this score, de Beauvoir contends that critics like Merleau-Ponty ignore the importance of intersubjectivity in his philosophy: "Against *Nausea, Being and Nothingness*, against everything Sartre has written, he maintains that Sartre's philosophy acknowledges nothing between subject and being-in-itself" (de Beauvoir, 1998: 452).

It is de Beauvoir's contention that even in Sartre's early works, one must come to terms with the fact that Sartre's philosophy is one in which time, history and politics are intersubjective poles that are equiprimordial and prior to the development of the "subject." Thus, the critiques of Merleau-Ponty and others such as Marcuse, whose focus is also on Sartre's early works, that

Sartre's philosophy is guilty of excessive subjectivity, simply fail to take into account the radical nature of Sartre's doctrine of Intentionality. As outlined very early in his philosophical development, and as underscored in the doctrine of the Intentionality of consciousness, it is overstated. Given the significance of the relationship between consciousness and world, and the structure of consciousness itself (that it is prior to the subject), the statement that Sartre's philosophy evinces an excessive subjectivity seems misplaced if for no other reason than that the subject is subsequent to a consciousness comprised of an existential field of relationships.[17] As de Beauvoir notes: "The psyche and the Ego which is its pole, are construed (constituted) by consciousness as objects."[18]

For de Beauvoir, Sartre's critics ignore the fact that consciousness and world are given in, as he puts it, "one felt swoop." There is more to this point than is usually admitted. According to de Beauvoir, the critique of Sartre's philosophy as subjectivism ignores Sartre's doctrine of Intentionality itself, in that Sartre is working with a revised version of Heidegger's being-in-the-world, albeit one that posits something anathema to Heidegger—consciousness, that shuns the formulation of subjectivity and objectivity in favor of a prior relationship to the world. By the self same argument that establishes consciousness as prior to and more foundational than the ego, Sartre's argument is that being-in-the-world (consciousness as for-itself), is prior and more foundational than notions of subjectivity and objectivity and their various derivations, such as subjectivism. "Consciousness," de Beauvoir contends, "and its pure presence to itself, is not a subject." And, furthermore: "On this basis Sartre has built his entire theory of the psychical field."[19] It is perhaps easy to overlook de Beauvoir's point concerning intersubjectivity in Sartre's philosophy, but perhaps this is not merely because of the emphasis on subjectivity that many of Sartre's critics have chosen to make the focus of their analysis. Instead, it may lie in the fact that the often-unacknowledged basis upon which intersubjectivity hinges, and indeed a great deal of Sartre's philosophy, involves a very precise delineation of the doctrine of Intentionality.

There is an additional point made by de Beauvoir regarding intersubjectivity, and it is directly related to the connection between intersubjectivity and Sartre's version of Realism: "The unveiling of the world, performed in the dimension of intersubjectivity, reveals realities which resist consciousness and possess their own laws. It is difficult to know what Merleau-Ponty means by *own energy*. But what is certain is that he insinuates that in Sartre intersubjective realities exist and relate to one another only through a subjectivity which supports them; whereas in Sartre, when he defined existential psychoanalysis, wrote: 'The meaningful, because of the very structure of transcendence, is a reference to other transcendents which can be interpreted without

recourse to the subjectivity which has established it.'"[20] Viewed from the perspective of Sartre's Realism, it does seem to be the case that the kind of Intentional field that Sartre posits presupposes the existence of Others.

De Beauvoir also defends Sartre against the charge of subjectivism by in-
voking Sartre's depiction of ideology. This is a noteworthy point since it is
generally Sartre's later works that are the focus for both supporters and detractors of his analysis of ideology. Yet, de Beauvoir cites this quote from
Henri`Martin: "In other environments children are immediately thrust into
the ideology of their class, it enters them as the air they breathe; they read it
on things; they learn it with the language; they never think about it, but always through it, since it is this ideology which produces and governs ideas."
De Beauvoir further notes: "He recognizes the same energy in literature
whose periods are born without a recourse to subjectivity; one only needs to
read *What is Literature* to be convinced."[21]

It is important to also note that what Sartre is addressing here is the socialization process, a category that is generally assumed to have been the focus
of his more mature works. Our point here has been to stress the political implications of Sartre's Realism, its relationship to Intentionality, of course, and
the fact, finally, that, if read in this way, Sartre's philosophy contains a powerful but often latent critique of all aspects of the socialization process. *Ipso
facto* that critique is present in his earliest writings as well as in his later ones.

The next step in our analysis involves describing the manner in which the
intentionality of consciousness is both a phenomenological ontology even
while being grounded in a "lack." This paradox is described by Sartre in his
"Ontological Proof" in *Being and Nothingness*, to which this analysis now
turns.

INTENTIONALITY IN BEING AND NOTHINGNESS: SARTRE'S ARGUMENT IN THE "ONTOLOGICAL PROOF."

Sartre's mature argument for the Intentionality of consciousness begins with
the necessity of the transphenomenality of the being of the phenomenon; that
is to say, because consciousness is always consciousness of something, there
must be a being of the phenomenon.[22] From this Sartre argues that there are
two possibilities that present themselves to those "who wish to make being
depend on consciousness."[23] Either consciousness constitutes the being of its
object, or consciousness is fundamentally relational, involving a relationship
to transcendent being. Furthermore, it cannot be the case that consciousness
constitutes its object because consciousness, by definition for Sartre, is necessarily "other" to what it is conscious of. In other words, a "full presence,"

a characteristic of the object that is necessary, is precisely *not* consciousness. However, there is another option. Consciousness can be an absence. One example would be Heidegger's being-towards-death. Another would be certain forms of Eastern philosophy, where the absence or "lack" can be depicted as a "void." This can indeed serve as the basis of ontology. On this score, Sartre maintains that: "If being belongs to consciousness, the object is not in consciousness."[24] This was the point Sartre made earlier in his article on Intentionality. However, here Sartre is refining his critique of Husserlian phenomenology: "For Husserl, for example, the animation of the hyletic nucleus by the only intentions which can find their fulfillment in this *hyle* is not enough to bring us out of subjectivity."[25] He then adds: "The truly objectifying *intentions* are empty *intentions*, those which aim beyond the present subjective appearance at the infinite totality of the series of appearances" (ibid.). Sartre continues his argument by noting, as Husserlian phenomenology had shown, that the perceptions of consciousness of the object are given to consciousness one at a time, and never as a totality.[26] "Thus," Sartre reasons, "the being of the object is pure non-being. It is defined as a *lack*" (ibid). As noted earlier, it is, in fact, composed of nothing other than intention. Sartre then asks how it is possible "that non-being (can) be the foundation of being?"[27] Or, even more specifically with regard to the issue of Intentionality in Husserl and Sartre, "How can the absent, *expected* subjective become thereby the objective?" (Ibid). Sartre then acknowledges the fact that with regard to expectations, it is obviously true that something one looks forward to, or "a grief which I dread" evinces a certain "transcendence in immanence" (Ibid). However, this itself is possible only because there is a prior being, or a fact in and of itself. It is "a presence (first) and not an absence. Sartre then critiques a certain interpretation of the relationship between the objective and the subjective, according to which each necessarily implies the existence of the other. This is the dialectical approach of Hegel, which Sartre flatly rejects: "The objective will never come out of the subjective nor the transcendent from immanence, nor being from non-being" (Ibid).[28] The focus then switches again to Husserl, and Sartre repeats his earlier critique from the *Transcendence of the Ego*, according to which Husserl failed to apply the consequences of his phenomenology to their fullest, most real and radical expression. Indeed, Husserl does define consciousness "as a transcendence," but there is a problem in that account for Sartre. For, he argues that, "from the moment that he (Husserl) makes of the *noema* an *unreal*, a correlate of the *noesis*, a noema whose *esse* is *percipi*, he is totally unfaithful to his principle" (Ibid). This is because the noema must be ontological in some meaningful sense, or in a way that does not depend on subjectivity. If the noesis is the reality principle, so to speak, one is compelled to adopt the position that subjectivity is guarantor of the

reality of the object. Denying the actual reality, or full reality and its corre-
sponding ontological status to the noema, means that, for Sartre, Phenomenology is not a realism at all, and the latter is, as noted, Sartre's view of *the*
major accomplishment of Phenomenology. Finally, Sartre inserts his own interpretation of this issue, and he reiterates what has already been said with regard to the primacy of Intentionality: "Consciousness is consciousness of
something. This means that transcendence is the constitutive structure of consciousness; that is, that consciousness is born *supported by* a being which is
not itself. This is what we call the ontological proof" (Ibid). Sartre underscores the fact that he views the character of Intentionality as the decisive element here. He maintains that Husserl "misunderstood its essential character"
which he takes to be the following: "To say that consciousness is consciousness of something means that for consciousness there is no being outside of
that precise obligation to be a revealing intuition of something—i.e., of a transcendent being."[29] For Sartre, there are two errors that Husserl made in his depiction of Intentionality: First, "Not only does pure subjectivity, if initially
given, fail to transcend itself to posit the objective," but, secondly, "a 'pure'
subjectivity disappears." Finally, Sartre maintains, "consciousness (of being)
consciousness must be qualified in some way, and it can be qualified only as
revealing intuition or it is nothing."[30]

For Sartre, this implies a fundamental ontological challenge: "Absolute
subjectivity can be established only in the face of something revealed; immanence can be defined only within the apprehension of a transcendent."[31] Nor,
for example, is this a matter of knowledge, of how and under what auspices
one can have a knowledge of essences. It is, for Sartre, more fundamental. In-
voking Descartes, he maintains: "We are here on the ground of being, not of
knowledge." The issue for Sartre is that consciousness implies in its being a
non-conscious and transphenomenal being." "Appearance," in short, lays
"claim to *being*," and is "everywhere."[32]

It is worth noting that Sartre concludes the ontological proof by citing Heidegger, with whose explication of there-being (*Dasein*), he draws a comparison: "Certainly we could apply to consciousness the definition which Heidegger reserves for Dasein and say that it is a being such that in its being, its being
is in question."[33] One might think that Sartre's approach has too great an affinity to Heidegger's conception of being, especially in its formulation as fundamental ontology, he makes the following observation. However, anticipating
his forthcoming critique of Heidegger, Sartre provides the following caveat to
a too close of an association of his phenomenology with that of Heidegger:
"But it would be necessary to complete the definition (above) and formulate it
more like this: *Consciousness is a being such that in its being, its being is in
question, in so far as this being implies a being other than itself*" (ibid).

With regard to Intentionality and constitution in Husserl, one can, of course, avoid the issue entirely and simply note that for Husserl phenomenology was understood as a science that entailed the removal of the "real" world and let it go at that. However, on the other hand, for Sartre the whole purpose of Intentionality was to be found in the act of encountering the world in-situ, "over there," as he put it in his article on Intentionality, or in a corner somewhere.

An additional difference between Husserl and Sartre on Intentionality can be underscored by assessing each philosopher's judgment of history and how Intentionality is a factor in the relationship between history and phenomenology. However, once again, the question of history itself underscores the differences between Husserl's and Sartre's philosophies of constitution and phenomenology itself. The issue of history brings into relief the differences already noted between Husserl and Sartre, first, on exactly how the doctrine of Intentionality, including the idea of constitution in Husserl can be established in terms of its origin as a feature of human agency, and second, how Sartre's idea of the psychical field establish intersubjectivity, as was discussed above in de Beauvoir's defense of Sartre regarding the charge of solipsism. It may be useful at this juncture, by way of forecasting, to note that there will be advanced a three-fold argument that is pivotal for Sartre's political philosophy and which is grounded in his depiction of a phenomenological ontology that applies to the "I" as well as everything else. First, there is for Sartre an irreducible relationship between consciousness and the world (Sartre's realism); second, this relationship is itself incomprehensible without the "intersubjective" world (being-for "others"), and, finally, there is an intersection of transcendences such that one can speak of an implied engagement *with* others (Sartre's version of *Mit-sein*). The totality of these relationships comprises the original foundation of the self and may likewise be viewed as a position in which existence *per se* is a political category.[34]

THE ARGUMENT CONCERNING
THE MISREADING OF HUSSERL

We will now introduce an alternative reading of Husserl and Sartre with a view towards exploring the consequences of Sartrean Realism. First, we will consider Edie's analysis and defense of Husserl against Sartre's claim that Husserl's Transcendental "I" is tantamount to idealism. Edie begins by noting that Sartre and some Sartre scholars have overstressed the differences between Husserl and Sartre, especially with regard to the charge of "idealism" first made by Sartre against Husserl in *The Transcendence of the Ego*.

On this score it is important to note that Sartre's disagreement with Husserl was also formulated along the lines of a *pre-reflective cogito*. However, this formulation is also used by Sartre to help establish the priority of consciousness over that of the "subject" or the "I." The argument in Transcendence of the Ego is that consciousness of self, which he terms in Transcendence of the Ego the "unreflective consciousness" (which, as noted, will later become the *pre-reflective cogito* in Being and Nothingness), is not positional. Instead, it is for Sartre more aptly described as an intersection of different acts of intentionality and little else. The pre-reflective self is described by Sartre as pure spontaneity. In "Intentionality" Sartre maintains that it is "nothing but the outside of itself and (that) it is this absolute flight, this refusal to be substance which constitute it as a consciousness."[35] Sartre's strongest words on the topic are contained in the contrast he draws between the phenomenological account of consciousness and the philosophy of mind of the tradition. As he notes in *The Transcendence of the Ego*, "the phenomenological conception of consciousness renders the unifying and individualizing role of the I totally useless. It is consciousness, on the contrary, which makes possible the unity and the personality of my I (as noted, the transcendental I, therefore, has no *raison d'etre*")[36] Finally, Sartre maintains that: "The transcendental I is the death of consciousness. Indeed the existence of consciousness is an absolute because consciousness is consciousness of itself."[37]

Not only Husserl's transcendental "I," but the idea of the "me" of the traditional depiction of consciousness collapses into the horizon in which and around which these acts of intentionality coalesce. For Sartre, in order to take the doctrine of intentionality really seriously, one needs to be prepared to consider consciousness as itself a phenomena, which for Sartre means that "to be and to appear are one"[38]

Sartre is critical in particular of the idea in Husserl's work that there is a fundamental reference point, or an "I," that makes all of this possible. In fact, Sartre is critiquing the idea of the *cogito* as an originary phenomena instead of something which itself rests on a more basic phenomena still—the structure of intentionality itself.

Sartre takes up the issue of the self-reflective consciousness from the perspective of the *cogito*, and he does so within the context of further establishing his point that intentionality does away with the "I" of the tradition. He begins by recalling that Descartes and Husserl invoke the "I," and subsequently support it, by appealing to the faculty of memory. This is perhaps an appropriate context for discussing the analysis put forth by Edie, who posits a defense of Husserl on the issue of the Transcendental "I". Edie argues that with regard to the "Transcendental I" in Husserl there are in fact two formulations of this issue: "the two 'I' thesis." As Edie puts it at the outset of his argument:

"My purpose in writing this essay is to ague that, stripped of its pseudo-polemic and reduced to its bare bones, to its ultimate meaning, Sartre's surface disagreement with Husserl is merely factitious, a purely verbal and not a substantial dispute."[39]

In order to make his argument, Edie begins by noting that Sartre did not attend Husserl's lectures at the Sorbonne in 1929. From this he seems to deduce that Sartre was only acquainted with some but not all of Husserl's works. He maintains: "He (Sartre) began to become acquainted with Husserl, bought and read Emmanuel Levinas' new book, *Theorie de l'intuition dans phenom-enologie de Husserl*, and spent the next six years reading Husserl, particularly *Ideas I* and the *Cartesian Meditations*. From his footnotes it is clear that he also looked into *Formal and Transcendental Logic* and "Inner Time Consciousness," and perhaps a few other things, but did not delve as deeply into their arguments"[40]

Edie's defense of Husserl against Sartre then proceeds to note that the presentation of objects to perception means that: "The perceptual object is given to me as having other sides, different aspects which I am not just now perceiving but which I *could* perceive, which I may even now experience as being seen by other persons occupying positions vis-à-vis the object which I do not yet occupy. These are all perspectives on the *same object* which are not now presented to me but which *could* be so given if I were to stand where the others are standing. Much more is 'appresented' to us in any given object of perception at any one instance than is actually 'presented' from my own necessarily perspectival viewpoint."[41]

What is particularly noteworthy about this perspective on Husserl and Sartre is the emphasis it gives to agency in the case of Sartre.[42] For, while it is true that the "given" exerts enormous pull on the phenomenology of both Husserl and Sartre, the perception of consciousness in Sartre is established against the backdrop of Sartre's engagement with a fundamental, if not to say for many, *the* fundamental category of Heidegger's *Being and Time*—being-towards-death. The latter is a foundational intentional horizon both for *Dasein*, in the case of Heidegger, and consciousness, in the case of Sartre. The differences between Heidegger and Sartre on what some view as the ground of Intentionality is the subject of analysis in the following section of this analysis. However, it needs to be noted that with regard to Husserl and Sartre on the matter of Intentionality, Sartre's work was heavily influenced by Heidegger's analysis, a fact that is discernable, as noted earlier, in Sartre's critique of Husserl in the opening pages of *Being and Nothingness*—the ontological proof.

Sartre does not invoke the language of "the given" to refer to individual objects given to consciousness. That is a position far closer to that of Merleau-Ponty.

Instead, when Sartre invokes "the given," it is almost invariably in the context of "realism,"[43] as it is in the quote from the article on "Intentionality," where it is used to underscore the coeval nature of consciousness and world. For example, in "Intentionality" he states that: "Consciousness and world are given in one shot: exterior by essence to consciousness, the world is, by essence, relative to it."[44]

In addition, each philosopher has a different area of emphasis—Husserl, for example, in the passage from Ideas that Edie cites, is focusing on the positional aspects of the object and holds that it can have an infinite number of adumbrations; that is to say, whereas it may be said that Husserl also establishes the various adumbrations effected by the reduction on the *hyle*, this refers back to the idea of a Transcendental "I," at least in the view of Sartre.[45]

Sartre's emphasis, on the other hand, as noted above, is on a bi-furcated relationship between consciousness and world. Some key terms used by Sartre underscore and reflect a far more radical idea of "the given" than anything one finds in Husserl's writings. For example, when, in the passage cited above, Sartre speaks of the world as "exterior by essence to consciousness" and that the world is, by essence, relative to it, he is arguing that consciousness and world are not, thereby, two poles, one the positional object and the other the correlating "noematic pole" of, as Edie puts it, an "infinite number of possible acts of consciousness."[46] Instead, what Sartre is arguing for in the article on "Intentionality" is that consciousness is part of that world and that there exists no vehicle or means for "getting behind it," or from escaping from the fact that consciousness and world are "given" in such a way that not only is it the case that the world is not *in* consciousness, but that consciousness itself is actually *in* the world. The order, in other words, needs to be reversed in the case of Sartre, since it is not the position of objects relative to consciousness that is decisive, but rather it is that of consciousness to other objects it encounters in the world. In sum, there is an externalism in Sartre that marks an important distinction between the intentionality of Husserl and that of Sartre.

NOTES

1. Sartre, op.cit.,1970: 4-5.
2. Ibid.
3. Sartre, op. cit., 1966: 4.
4. Sartre, op. cit., 1991: 93.
5. Ibid.: 80-81.
6. Sartre, op. cit.,1966: 41.

7. Ibid.:594.

8. Sartre, op. cit., 1991: 40.

9. Ibid.

10. Sartre, op. cit., 1966: lxxii.

11. Ibid.: 150.

12. Ibid: 129.

13. Sartre, op.cit.,1991: 40.

14. This also provides an answer to a possible critique: How is it that Sartre's philosophy is intersubjective even while his work is interpreted as an explicit rejection of the subject as the ground of consciousness? The answer involves his formulation of intersubjectivity and the fact that it depends on a bifurcation, imminent to the world, of "Other" consciousnesses.

15. Sartre, op.cit., 1991: 41.

16. Simone de Beauvoir, "Merleau-Ponty and Pseudo Sartreanism" in Jon Stewart *The Debate Between Sartre and Merleau-Ponty*, ed. Jon Stewart (Evanston: Northwestern,1998: 449.

17. Sartre does address this issue himself in his section on "The Reef of Solipsism" in Being and Nothingness, where he goes to considerable lengths to establish the importance of being-with (*Mit-sein*). While not using the term "intersubjective" there are many passages in *Being and Nothingness* that are radically intersubjective. The discussion of "shame," for example, is a depiction of *Mit-Sein* as just such an illustration of radical intersubjectivity.

18. de Beauvoir, op. cit., 1998

19. Ibid.

20. de Beauvoir, op. cit., 1998: 456.

21. Ibid.

22. It is important to note that it is the interpretation of this premise that separates Sartre not only from Husserl, but from Heidegger as well. For, as Sartre notes a little further on in his argument: "If we wish to make being depend on consciousness the object must be distinguished not by presence," as, one can add, in Heidegger, "but by its *absence* (emphasis added)—not by its plentitude" (here one thinks of Husserl's hyletic nucleus and its adumbrations), but by its nothingness" (Sartre, 1966: lxxii).

23. Sartre, op. cit., 1966: lxxii.

24. Ibid.

25. Sartre, op. cit., 1966: lxxii.

26. Husserl had argued, of course, that the *epoche* is accomplished by way of an infinity of *possible* adumbrations or presentations. It can never, on principle, be exhausted, but only partly explicated or presented.

27. Sartre, op. cit., 1966: lxxiii.

28. Heidegger, in his analysis of Hegel's Phenomenology, effects a variation on this position. Hegel had declared in his Logic that Being is empty, even the most empty of concepts (a statement reproduced at the onset of Being and Time), and that both Being and Nothing receive actual content only in the concept of "Becoming." Heidegger re-formulates this as having as its actual meaning Heidegger's own concept of Being.

29. Sartre, op. cit.,

30. Ibid

31. Ibid.

32. Ibid.

33. Ibid.: lxiv).

34. This position is explicitly put forth in Sartre's plays such as The Flies. An exposition of this text is included in the section on politics that concludes this study. Here, it may suffice to note that In The Flies there is nothing explicitly political that Orestes does that is threatening to King or Deity. Orestes' mere existence as a "free man" is what sets up a state of derived political strife. In sum, authenticity is a political category for Sartre; it does not have this character for Heidegger.

35. (Sartre, op. cit., 1970: 4-5.

36. Sartre, op. cit., 1991: 40.

37. Ibid.

38. Ibid.:42.

39. James Edie, "The Question of the Transcendental Ego: Sartre's Critique of Husserl," in *Existentialist Ontology and Human Consciousness*, ed. McBride (New York: Garland,1997): 87.

40. Ibid.: 88.

41. Ibid.: 89.

42. However, this inference seems to contradict the basic argument of the essay in that what Edie is arguing is precisely this: That one cannot, and indeed in the case of Husserl, should not, merely look at a single work of a thinker, but instead one should consider the full sweep of their analyses and contributions in order to fashion a critique. In this instance, Edie seems to be arguing that a series of lectures by Husserl, and not even a text, should be given special prominence.

43. Here the word "realism" refers to the world as given; that is to say, as phenomenal. For Sartre, the real world as given includes objects and "Others" as they are presented to consciousness, and for this reason, the realism of Sartre includes the intersubjective world.

44. (Sartre, op.cit., 1970: 4-5).

45. In his analysis of history Husserl diminishes this emphasis somewhat by his depiction of the *life-world*. However one must consider the various issues of contestation within Husserlian scholarship.

46. Edie, op. cit., 1997: 95.

Chapter Four

What is Bad Faith?

The reality behind Sartre's concept of bad faith is historical and so it it was not discovered by Sartre. Instead, it was his genius to give the name to a phenomenon that was spoken about in some of our most ancient texts and by almost all of the ancient writers. It refers to the mostly hidden field of human intention including one's intention towards oneself. For example, the books of the Old Testament and many of the teachings of Jesus refer to phenomenon according to which one acts in a purely fine way but nevertheless has a kind of malice in their heart. Similarly, in the Eastern tradition, as D.T. Suzuki noted in many of his works, there are strong proscriptions against this kind of duplicity. But bad faith is not only about the malice that may exist in one's heart, it is something else that Sartre has as his focus, and it is this second aspect of bad faith that serves as the link between politics and ontology. It is a pretense wherein one acts and believes or tries to, that one is made of the same stuff as what one is conscious of, or in other words, that one is a thing. It is a deliberate negation of the awareness of human freedom and is thereby, according to Sartre the basic malady that makes all of the others possible. Sartre uses the analogy of a stone and says that in bad faith one wants sometimes desperately to escape the freedom on consciousness by acting as though they are a stone, or something that is essentially fixed and solid. Eric Fromm preferred the language of armor but whatever analogy one uses the key idea is a kind of betrayal of one's own spirit. There is an intuitive as well as an experiential appeal to what Sartre has to say about bad faith and so before proceeding it may be useful to provide some ready examples of the concept *in situ*. Sartre loved to use the example of lovers to explicate his concepts and so we can imagine the condition of two lovers one of whom has adopted bad faith. There is nothing explicitly wrong with their outward behavior perhaps but as the poets and songwriters have always said nevertheless something essential is wrong. Love is gone and what is left in its place is a contract, a ring perhaps or various activities. Such a condition is informed by the existence of bad faith for one of the parties is attempting to act as though their freedom has been replaced by the formal accoutrements of love. Parental love also provides an excellent illustration of bad faith for parents will frequently comment on how they could discern the bad faith of their children even though to all outward appearances everything "seemed fine." Despite its appeal and seeming ease, bad faith is actually a difficult feat to pull off for one's existence seeks freedom in every instance and in bad faith one is replacing that freedom with a façade and so it represents the ultimate internal conflict only it is not internal it is external in the sense that it is affliction of one's being-in-the-world. Still another example is that of the bureaucrat who has adopted a bad faith approach to a client, in this instance all of the formalities ma be present but small details may be withheld, delays and so forth. If we continue along the line that leads from the individual to the family or group to society we can use the following example of bad faith at the social level of analysis even though it is always undertaken by individuals. Theresa Fucicello, in her work, The Tyranny of Kindness the author recalls her days of dependency on charitable institutions and how despite the offerings that were proffered to her invariably there was also a good deal of what Sartre terms bad faith doled out as well. An attitude of superiority informed those who provided the goods, money or services and the existential correlative be it in the form of a gesture, a tone of voice or an innuendo was the likely verification. Finally, at the historical level of analysis there is the example of the freedom rides through the American South during the Civil Rights movement in which bad faith was exposed in a violent, tragic and unequivocal way. The rides themselves were organized because African-Americans lived the daily experience of racism in the South and yet were met with the tactic of official denial. So, the idea was that by simply acting as free individuals and riding a bus through the deep South they would be committing a stigmatized act and as we know, the freedom riders called forth all of the venomous bad faith of White supremacy and racism that constituted the "really real." There are of course many other examples that may be cited to explicate Sartre's concept of bad faith but these should serve to introduce the concept.

The focus will now be placed on establishing the connection that Sartre makes between bad faith and realism. This is an important connection for two reasons. First, the linkage itself is a continuation of the critique of the "Transcendental I;" that is to say, because the "I," or subject, is generally considered the ultimate source of freedom, it is important to show that there is an activity in which the freedom of the subject is derivative of a more primordial freedom. Bad faith is an illustration of this point. In effect, bad faith is a negative argument for existential or phenomenological freedom over the freedom of the subject sometimes derided by Sartre as *freedom of the will*. Secondly, bad faith is also a bridge between philosophy and politics, including the politics of socialization and "reification." For Sartre, bad faith is the primary form of "reification," its template, so to speak, and serves thereby as the ground for other forms and expressions of "reification." On this score, as we will see in the example of anti-Semitism, one of Sartre's contributions to philosophy in general and political philosophy in particular, is an intersubjective account of consciousness and, consequently, ideology as well. Here we are using Marx's concept of ideology where the term refers to ideas and systems of ideas that are used to obscure political interest often through the use of abstract categories (such as universal political interest) in place of history and historical analysis.

The link, or connection, then, between the social and political level of analysis and that of individual consciousness is the phenomenon of bad faith. This is not to say that Reality is apolitical in the first instance, but rather that the positing of bad faith, and one's engaging in it, is precisely the negation of the freedom of consciousness as Sartre understands it. The world may very well be "reified," but for Sartre it does not follow that one must thereby also act in bad faith. Conversely, one can be in possession of an accurate appraisal of Reality and still infect one's self with and through bad faith.

Bad faith is, however, more than a bridge to Sartre's later political writings. It is also Sartre's depiction of a sub-species of alienation: that of self-alienation. On this score, it may be useful to say a word, even if briefly, about the topic and Sartre's place in the history of its depiction.

First, there have been a number of approaches to alienation and ideology that have borrowed from the Freudian tradition with its emphasis on "repression." Here, Marcuse's analysis of alienation is particularly relevant. Secondly, there are Heideggerian or neo-Heideggerian approaches to alienation that are specifically traceable to those sections of *Being and Time* that treat the phenomenon of *Das Mann*. These have surfaced in popular culture in films and in novels, as well as in theological studies such as that of Paul Tillich and others. However interesting, we will not consider the Heideggerian account of alienation here. Suffice it to say that Heidegger's analysis is part of a long tradition that includes, perhaps most significantly, the contributions of Kierkegaard. The other important tradition on this topic is that of Freud's analysis. A more sustained consideration of the thesis of "repression" will be introduced shortly. The point that should be introduced here, however, is this: Freud's depiction of the structure of repression, including the fact that it is inextricably intertwined with the creation, maintenance and reproduction

of the social order may be viewed as providing the basis for several approaches to the study and depiction of alienation. One that of Herbert Marcuse, involves making a distinction between repression *per se*, the kind of
transhistorical Reality that is part and parcel of all societies, and what Marcuse terms *surplus repression*. *Surplus repression* is the kind of repression
that is tied to a technological society, one that is Capitalist, and as such is informed by the presence of an ideology of *performance*.

However, another route that leads from the Freudian concept of repression
and its contribution to alienation is the one chosen by Sartre. This approach
involves revisiting the concept of repression itself and the posing of the question of whether there might be a more basic phenomenon that serves as the
basis for repression. The by-now familiar formulation of consciousness as
grounded in a "lack," and a bifurcation between consciousness as in-itself and
a for-itself is, for Sartre, this more primordial basis.

A related difficulty is the one that has been present from the outset of our
analysis and that is, of course, the issue of the difficulty of determinism generally because, , on this score, the Freudian notion of repression denies the
position that Sartre argues: That freedom as one's only essence means that
one is also responsible for their actions, and the Freudian terminus of the self
in a natural impulse, or that of an inner conflict between internalized socialization (the ego and the superego), appears to leave open the possibility of an
escape from freedom, if not responsibility. It will be recalled that Freud's argument, especially in *Civilization and its Discontents,* is that the sexual energy, or *libido,* must be held in check in order for civilization, not only to
flourish, but even to be. The tension, as it is often enough portrayed, is between the ego and the id, the latter of which possesses often antisocial impulses. Here, it is important to note a significant qualification and that is that
Sartre, including his early works, is not denying the existence of and role
played by the socialization process broadly defined. Instead, what he takes issue with is the more circumscribed view that these structures are secondary
to a more basic Reality—the Intentionality of consciousness.

On this score, Sartre offers a rival theory of the emotions; one could say
that Sartre's critique of ideology underscores his position that repression is an
epi-phenomenon of ideology. It is not an essence of the self and as such it
does not imply the existence of an essentialized tripartite self, of course, let
alone the characteristics of a substrate that gives rise to consciousness. What
can, ultimately, be quantified, predicted, and tested is the subject, which, as
we have already seen, is derived from consciousness and not the reverse.
Even here we see that Sartre's philosophy, which is grounded in his depiction
of Intentionality, remains a radical critique of essentialism. In so far as psy-
chologism, be it of Freudian psychoanalysis, or more currently, some of the

new forms of physiology, posits the view that there is a subject in *default* either through a lack of knowledge, or the correct balance of brain chemistry, it is mistaken. One must first acknowledge existence itself as comprised of a basic relationship to the world. The very fact that the subject must *present* seems to suggest that consciousness is prior. One argument that is often advanced in this regard to refute human agency is that of psychopharmacology. A closer examination however, reveals the following support for Sartre's view. It is that one can, in fact see in the extraordinary usefulness of psychopharmacology that the biochemical foundation of mental illness obscures a still more fundamental fact: the *agency* of the individual in deciding to view their mental state in that way (as opposed to denial), and to seek a solution. In cases of extreme mental illness, of course, 'others' make this decision, but the *fact* of human agency is still decisive and foundational.

For Sartre's the idea of Realism extends to the emotions and it is in this area that the radical nature of his Realism appears most distinctly. Here the analysis is using "realism" in the sense in which Sartre uses it in his first account of the topic: his article on "Intentionality." In this view, "realism" refers to an axis that also includes "idealism," both of which comprise one of the perennial problems of philosophy within the philosophical tradition. On the one hand his analysis is tantamount to a critique of traditional 'realism', according to which the mind receives ideas based on actually present correlates in the natural world. However, on the other hand, Sartre is also critical of a second form of realism in which case the Realism at issue is grounded in the existence of an essential human core, be it the *id, ego, superego* of the Freudian tradition, or the "I" of the philosophical tradition in the West. In response to the these 'realisms' Sartre proposes, through his argument for the intentionality of consciousness, an alternative that is based on, as he puts it in his article on "Intentionality," *the rupture in being* that comprises the most primary fact about the human condition.

The theory of the emotions, therefore, is both an aspect of Sartre's theory of Intentionality and also a significant critique of other versions of Realism, especially those noted above. It is also in this context that Sartre's philosophy, if not dealing finally with the issue raised by McCulloch of 'pseudo' objects, at the very least enriches it by positing another media by which to delineate the 'real' vs. the pseudo-object.

As has been the case throughout this analysis, the guide to Sartre's theory of the emotions will be the concept of intentionality, especially as that doctrine was formulated by Sartre early in the development of his philosophy. For, as Mazis notes: "We can see how Sartre's earlier work, *The Transcendence of the Ego*, is vital to understanding his work on the emotions." [1] Mazis cites the following passage, one that he considers a key text for Sartre's theory of the emotions, from *The Transcendence of the Ego*, "The phenomenologists have plunged man back into the world; they have given full measure to man's agonies and sufferings, and also to his rebellions. Unfortunately, as long as the *I* remains a structure of absolute consciousness, one will still be able to reproach phenomenology for being an escapist doctrine, for pulling man out of the world, and in that way, turning our attention from the real problems. It seems to us that this reproach no longer has any justification if one makes the *me* an existent strictly contemporaneous with the world, whose existence has the same essential characteristics of the world."[2]

But if human existence is "contemporaneous with the world" then the question of discerning the differences between the apparently real and the 're-ally' real becomes all the more pressing. On this score, it should be said that for Sartre, the primary deception that the individual must deal with is the is-sue of *bad faith*. The latter is considered by Sartre during the course of his analysis of Freud's theory of repression and the unconscious. As noted, the analysis of Freud is important because it provides an excellent illustration of his point concerning the priority of Intentionality over what he argues are sec-ond-order phenomena, however, it an important caveat here is that it is very easy to overstate the differences between Freud and Sartre. There is a great deal of Freud's analysis that Sartre accepts. For example, one of his criticisms of Heidegger is that he totally ignores the importance of human sexuality as a dimension of *Mit-Sein*. It is the issue of repression that is the focus of Sartre's disagreement. For Sartre there is no question as to where one should begin the analysis of Freud: It must center on the idea of repression and self-deception, which Sartre views as of secondary importance to the Intentional-ity of consciousness and bad faith respectively. The latter are ontological, the former are ontic. Here we are using 'ontic' and 'ontological' as terms to de-note not only a different structural level—the ontological referring to the most basic statements one can make about the individual, but also to refer to the fact that one is temporally prior—the Intentionality of consciousness and the capacity for adopting a bad faith comportment towards one's existence are given a birth prior to the establishment of complexes and repression, or even the tripartite structure of *id, ego, and superego*. However, initially, there does seem to be a contradiction in what Sartre has to say about deception. For, al-though Sartre critiques the idea that one can lie to oneself, a complex argu-ment that will be considered separately, he is in accord with the idea that, pre-cisely because the external world is real and is experienced on its own terms, one can err in one's discernment of it. One can, in strictly formal terms, be in bad faith about one's identity, and subsequently establish a second order nar-rative that reflects this. As Sartre notes in his discussion of bad faith: "It is best to choose and to examine one determined attitude which is essential to human reality and which is such that consciousness instead of directing its negation outwards turns it in toward itself. This attitude, it seems to me, is *bad faith.*"[3] One can, in short, be wrong, and proceed wrongly in any number of ways based upon the information one received concerning the world. However, according to Sartre, what one cannot be mistaken concerning, is the fact that one is in possession of certain information either about oneself or one's motives. That said, Sartre does agree that this creates certain difficulties and conflicts for the individual, and these difficulties can lead an individual to psychoanalysis. As he puts it: "To escape from these difficulties (of facing existential truths), people gladly have recourse to the unconscious. In the psychoanalytic interpretation, for example, they use the hypothesis of the censor, conceived as a line of demarcation with customs, passport division, currency control, etc., to re-establish the duality of the deceiver and deceived. Here instinct or, if you prefer, original drives and complexes of drives constituted by our individual history, make up *reality*" (Sartre, 1966: 61)

INTENTIONALITY AND THE EMOTIONS

The radicalism of Sartre's approach to Realism surfaces not only in his elucidation of the faculty of the imagination, but in his depiction of the emotions as well. In terms of our procedure here, the most relevant aspects of his theory of the emotions concerns his engagement with Freud. This is because his analysis of Freud centers on the question of repression, of course, as well as the fact that for Sartre existential freedom requires a direct encounter with one's own psychic life. So, while for both Freudian psychoanalysis and existential psychoanalysis, the 'things' that are referred to consciousness are, in fact, real, in the case of the latter access to this sequence of what is real requires a mediator. A second question that will be addressed is that of whether or not the individual's mental states are exhausted by naturalized Reason. This is a topic of considerable debate within contemporary philosophy and so, however compelling it is as an issue between Freud and Sartre and their respective accounts of Realism, we will for the most part restrict our analysis here to a consideration of the issue of repression. The thinking behind this judgment is that our goal here is the exposition of the relationship between Realism and freedom in Sartre, and we have already established the fact that for Sartre, since consciousness is grounded in a "lack," *ipso facto* one of its products, Reason, cannot be naturalized.

We should begin our consideration of Realism from the perspective of the emotions by recalling the realism that Sartre sees in emotional states. For Sartre: "Fear, forgetting, dreams really exist in the capacity of concrete facts of consciousness in the same way as the words and attitudes of the liar are concrete, really existing patterns of behavior. The subject has the same relation to these phenomena as the deceived to the deceiver" (Ibid). One might be led to ask why it is that Sartre uses the analysis of lying to Others as an introduction to a critique of Freud. Here one issue is that of methodology which wile it is somewhat less relevant when viewed in the overall context (i.e. self deception), nevertheless serves to differentiate Sartre's from Freud's in that Sartre's approach, as ontological, is literally the more radical in the literal sense. However, with respect to the specific critique of the censor, the issue of "method," because it implies ontology, is somewhat more pertinent. For, one of the main advantages of Sartre's analysis is that it offers one a vantage point within the traditional dichotomies such as 'nature' or 'nurture,' that of being-in-the-world, from which to critique subsequently derived narratives of the self and society. The answer to this question is Sartre's use of a phenomenological methodology. For, Sartre uses his own version of a phenomenological reduction in order to set off the ordinary lie over and against the kind of lying that goes on in self-deception. This affords Sartre the opportunity to carry on a phenomenological reduction of the process of deception *per se*. For Sartre begins with the most mundane and apparent instances under investigation, in this case the everyday lie, and then moving on to increasingly deeper and more complex instances of deception. Indeed, as scholars have noted, one can point to a specific methodology at work in his critique of the idea of the unconscious. The upshot is that Sartre has a more focused critique. For, as Catalano notes in his analysis of self-deception, the sequence of Sartre's argument in Being and Nothingness matters a great deal, for much of Sartre's argument hinges on bad faith which is placed early in the overall text so as to provide the logical groundwork for what follows. This is, he argues especially the case with regard to the critique of of the idea of repression. The work, in other words is connected through the strong case Sartre makes for bad faith.

One can see this point more clearly in Sartre's subsequent delineation of the reduced 'essence' of self-deception. In that context, when, during the course of psychoanalysis, the analyst begins to discover the symbolic truth of deception (which truth is accounted in that in order for the deception involved in self-deception to be true, *qua* deception, it must be so in a mediated sense). It is this that the analyst discovers. Indeed, what makes this phenomena self-deceptive from a phenomenological point of view, is something quite different from the ordinary view. That is, an often overlooked basis of Sartre's critique of Freud and the entire edifice of the symbolic interpretation of consciousness is his retrieval of Husserl's idea of originary perception as the ground of both the natural and the phenomenological perspective. This is apparent in Sartre's formulation of the problem: "Thus the subject deceives

himself about the *meaning* of his conduct; he apprehends it in its concrete existence but not in its *truth*, simply because he cannot derive it from an original situation."[4]

One contrast that Sartre makes here is with the three-fold formulation of
id, ego and, eventually, *super-ego*. For Sartre, Freudian psychoanalysis di-
vides the psychic individual into two. Furthermore, it is the function of the
analyst to be the 'Other' or mediator between the *id* and the *ego*. "The dis-
covery," of the truth about oneself, Sartre tells us, will necessitate the cooperation of the psychoanalyst, who appears as the *mediator* between my unconscious drives and my conscious life. The 'Other' appears to be able to
induce the synthesis between the unconscious thesis and the conscious an-
tithesis. One can know oneself in terms of motivation only through the mediation of the 'Other,' which means that I stand in relation to *my* 'id', in the
position of the *Other*" (Ibid). In short, what psychoanalysis accomplishes, according to Sartre, is the phenomenon of the lie without the liar. Before proceeding further it should be noted that not all Freudian scholars accept
Sartre's portrayal of psychoanalysis. Marcuse, for example, in *Eros and Civilization* contends that the *id* is unlike the other structures of the psyche that,
in the latter's view, come into being through a kind of being-in-the-world.
For example, there is in Marcuse's view a fundamental conflict between the
life instinct and the death instinct that is grounded in a fundamental relationship to the world. However, the emphasis that Marcuse places on history in
his reading of Freud's analysis has the effect of rendering the individual's
psyche, if not the life of the human species, far more susceptible to historical
influence than the one Freud offers.[5]

The duality that Sartre discussed in his analysis of ordinary lying to an
'Other,' is reintroduced by the analyst by the device of unconscious drives or
complexes. Unlike ordinary lying the place of oneself and the 'Other' is
switched with that of the *id* and the *ego*. Sartre maintains that "it introduces
into my subjectivity the deepest intersubjective structure of the *Mit-sein*."[6]

Sartre continues this part of his analysis by considering the phenomenon of
resistance, wherein the patient exhibits defiance by refusing to speak or provides astounding but untrue accounts of their dreams or drops out of psychoanalytic treatment totally. So, Sartre asks us to consider what exactly is it in
one that can resist? The point that Sartre is stressing here is that this idea of
the censor is untenable from a logical point of view. For, it involves the thesis that it must both know what to keep hidden (implying knowledge), while
at the same time not knowing, since to know would be to have full consciousness. This is because, first, within the Freudian framework, the judg-
ments of any of the parts have not been established in such a manner that one
can say with any degree of certainty that any particular judgment is true. It

should also be noted, of course, that one can adopt a phenomenological approach towards the idea of the unconscious in which case the repression, somewhat transparent to the analysis but hidden from the subject, only appears when it is an 'object' *for* consciousness. Such an interpretation of Freud's thesis concerning the unconscious would solve some problems, but invariably open up others, since, at the end of the day; it is the existence of specific symptoms that underscores the presence of repression. The best one can hope for in this approach to self-analysis is the correspondence of the subject's eventual perspective on the meaning of his behavior with that of the analyst (a state of affairs that is troubling for Sartre). Furthermore, it appears that the proceedings are conducted along the lines of a working hypothesis, wherein the explanation that explains the most behavior is considered the best and most accurate analysis. But even here, Sartre argues, the psychoanalyst needs the full cooperation of the censor because only the censor knows the details of any repression. Again, for Sartre this seems fraught with difficulties since, as just noted, the structures of the self, in models of the self that have recourse to the idea of the unconscious, have failed to provide the kind of certainty that one experiences in intuitive truth. For Sartre, this is a fundamentally different quality to the truth that one receives about oneself phenomenologically and that which is merely possible or conjectural, or even hypothetical. Unlike the 'working hypothesis' of the psychoanalyst, the 'reality' about oneself has the *imprimatur* of existence itself, it has its own reality, or the weight of being real, as it is sometime put. There is a texture to the 'real' because consciousness, as intentional, is among the 'real,' or at the 'real', and relates to it on the basis of involvement, as a being-in.

Sartre further considers the idea of the 'censor,' and argues that it presents an additional difficulty and that is that the censor so depicted seems to use judgment regarding what is or is not to be repressed and there can be no other conclusion but that there is some deliberation involved. For, on the one hand, lawful sexual impulses are allowed to pass through to consciousness but mysteriously unlawful ones are repressed. For Sartre, the contradiction that lies at the heart of the Freudian conception of the psyche is reducible to this: How can we sign on to the device of the censor when its very existence involves a "knowledge that is ignorant of itself." Sartre's depiction of the 'censor' is that: "It must be the consciousness of being conscious of the drive to be repressed, but precisely *in order not to be conscious of it.*" This is tantamount, in Sartre's view, to a definition of *bad faith* itself.[7]

In this section of the analysis we will continue to examine the phenomenon of bad faith as an application of Sartre's theory of Intentionality. This is because it represents a key text for Sartre's phenomenology since it is tantamount to a detailed exposition of the more formal an abstract argument presented in *The Transcendence of the Ego* regarding how it that human existence is unique in terms of agency. On the other hand, within the context of the argument set out in *Being and Nothingness*, bad faith helps to delineate the major theme of the 'ontological proof.' That is to say, bad faith s possible only because of the bifurcation or duality of the *in-itself* and the *for-itself*.

The point of origin for Sartre's doctrine of Bad faith takes is the Intentionality of consciousness. It is as both in-itself and for-itself, immanence and transcendence. On this score, Sartre's argument for the priority of bad faith over other accounts of human intention, a logical one. This is the case even though the illustrations that Sartre uses to explicate it, such as that of dating, or the performance of a waiter in a café, are drawn from the everyday. In fact, the style of Sartre's argument involves a logical inquiry, as we saw above in the discussion of repression, where Sartre's focus in that portion of his analysis was specifically on the logic embedded in the idea of the censor according to which, again, it must *both* know what to censor and not know, since otherwise it would be fully aware or conscious, followed by a phenomenological description, as outlined earlier by Catalano. The logic of argumentation, however, is supplemented by what appears to be anecdotal evidence. In fact though, what is entailed by this procedure is a phenomenological description or an exposition of the necessary ideas behind any given set of actions. What Sartre is attempting to do in the critique of repression and the delineation of bad faith is to establish social reality at a more fundamental and primary level of analysis. That is, one that is phenomenological. One can object, of course that Freud grounds his theory in the natural order, and, therefore, it could be argued that one could hardly look for a more fundamental level of analysis than that of the biology of sexual impulses and urges. For Sartre, the logic of the immediately given, the very literal definition of phenomenology itself, is prior to the structures of the self and its delineation as being fundamentally, a biological given. The biology of the body, in other words, is first of all rooted in a biology of being-in-the-world socially and historically as *praxis* and individually and developmentally as a relational ontology to Others, objects and states. By contrast, for Sartre, the given as being-in-the-world, because it is established at once with one's existence remains the primary and fundamental fact. It is, on that account the most fundamental level of analysis. Sartre's point then can be phrased as follows: Traditional psychoanalysis is a de-ontology.

We can see this slightly differently if we consider the following formulation. Sartre could have availed himself of the concept of the *self-fulfilling prophecy*. Had he done so, his critique of psychoanalysis on the basis of freedom and awareness would have been more succinct. For, he could have argued that the *self-fulfilling prophecy* is antithetical to the idea of repression and determinism, can give rise, on the part of the individual, to any number of psychological manifestations including that of 'repression' and its derived concepts such as 'transference', 'sublimation' and 'displacement'. Such a procedure would make for an exceedingly powerful social critique that was completely grounded in a theory of alienation.

Sartre begins his discussion of bad faith by defining it as a phenomenon wherein one treats one's status as an immanence as a transcendence; and one's status as a transcendence as an immanence. He cites the exploitation of this rupture or negation between the two as fundamental for the phenomenon of bad faith in that the human being is one that can adopt a deliberate negative attitude with respect to oneself. The discussion of bad faith proceeds from this fundamental capacity for negation and during the course of his analysis he cites the example of the master-slave relationship, in which the reality of the slave encounters its own possibility as a negation in the form of a master. However, this same negation at an ontological level can occur when consciousness effects a negation of its most significant bifurcation, that of consciousness as for-itself and in-itself. Bad faith is this condition. Sartre maintains that one sees this negation at work in other human endeavors, in the use of irony, for example. For in irony, one posits a statement that is, at the same time, is the negation of what was just posited. Thus, for example, when Sophocles has Oedipus make himself blind, what is in fact being posited is the exact opposite: Now, for the first time, Oedipus sees.

THE DOCTRINE OF BAD FAITH AS A
NEGATIVE ARGUMENT FOR FREEDOM

Sartre undertakes a phenomenological step back at several points in his argument for the basic freedom of consciousness. The exposition of the doctrine of bad faith illustrates this. We can, for example, observe this when we inquire about an individual who can deny himself to himself. First, however, it needs to be said that generalized self-negation is too broad. That it exists under many modalities is abstractly obvious, and as the example of irony illustrates, it can find its way into numerous human endeavors. Instead, for Sartre, what is called for is a specific form of self-negation, that of bad faith. Bad faith is a negation but although negation is usually a phenomenon that is directed towards the outside world, is instead turned inward on one's self. It is coupled with an attitude of pretense about both the negative perception and the pretense. On this score, one question that Sartre anticipates involves the relationship, if any, between lying and bad faith.

In the instance of a lie, "consciousness affirms that it exists by nature as *hidden from the other*; it utilizes for its own profit the ontological duality of myself and myself in the eyes of the other. The situation cannot be the same for bad faith if this, as we have said, is indeed a lie to oneself. To be sure the one who practices bad faith is hiding a displeasing truth or presenting as truth a pleasing untruth. Bad faith then has in appearance the structure of false-hood. Only what changes everything is the fact that in bad faith it is from my-self that I am hiding the truth. Thus, the duality of deceiver and deceived does not exist here. Bad faith on the contrary implies in essence the unity of a *single* consciousness. This does not mean that it cannot be conditioned by the *Mit-sein* like all other phenomena of human reality, but the *Mit-sein* can call forth bad faith only by presenting itself as *a situation* which bad faith permits surpassing; bad faith does not come from outside to human reality. One does not undergo bad faith; one is not infected with it; it is not a *state*. But consciousness infects itself with bad faith. There must be an original intention and a project of bad faith; this project implies a comprehension of bad faith as such and a pre-reflective apprehension (of) consciousness as affecting it-self with bad faith."[8]

Earlier, we saw that it is because of the opacity of consciousness to itself that the idea of repression is antithetical to Sartre's phenomenological ontol-ogy. However, there is another facet to this point and it is this: Just as one can exploit the bifurcation of consciousness and lie to the Other, but not to one's self, at least formally, so too one's capacity as *Mit-sein*, a being-with, can be exploited as a component of bad faith. For example, one can use Others and *Mit-sein* as an *a priori* structure of one's own being-in-the-world to hide one's own freedom. This, in essence, is the core of Sartre's critique of Heidegger's account freedom. In another context, however, bad faith can be seen from the vantage point of the relationship between Intentionality and time. From this vantage point, *Mit-sein* which, which again, Sartre takes pains to point out is not an *a priori* feature of consciousness, entails the development of layers of the moments of Intentionality. Consequently, one can point to a social di-mension in which the awareness of the existence of *bad faith* is an important foundation for the accuracy of perception. Sartre's doctrine, tantamount to a critical Intentionality, is a first step in deciphering ideologies. For, under-standing the ontology that is at work in bad faith is, in fact essential for es-tablishing the parameters of determining second-level, systematic deceptions, structural *scarcity*, and the reification of consciousness as expressions of alienation. In sum, delineating and coming to terms with bad faith represents an epistemological threshold that Sartre believes a philosophy must meet in order for it to be truly realist.[9] This is true whether or not one is speaking of the early works such as the article on "Intentionality," the study of Husserl's phenomenology, *The Transcendence of the Ego*, the larger work, *Being and Nothingness*, or even the later work, *Critique of Dialectical Reason* (where Sartre switches to the terminology of dialectics and relies on the phenomenon of reification to make a number of similar points). This is because for Sartre, ultimately, human existence is structured in such a way that, strictly speaking, the capability to deceive oneself is more limited than it initially appears to be. The difference that needs to be underscored is that which pertains to the practicality of bad faith (its reality within mundane existence), and its status as a possible human condition. For, it is only by dint of appearance that one is acting in bad faith. For, strictly speaking, in Sartre's view, bad faith is by definition knowledge that it is taking place. One can see this more clearly when one considers that the discussion of *bad faith* that proceeds from Sartre's analysis of the phenomenology of lying. It is a process in which Sartre moves the reader from a consideration of what takes place during the usual course of a lie, its mundane reality, to a consideration of what is, on the one hand a particular instance of lying—that whereby the individual lies to oneself, and one the other, the phenomenological essence of lying according to Sartre—the attempt to deceive oneself.

There are additional aspects to the relationship between bad faith and *Mit-sein*. Sartre draws attention to the everyday character of it and, in doing so exacerbates the contrast between his version of *Mit-sein* and that of Heidegger. For example, he notes in his discussion of lying that "The lie is also a normal phenomenon of what Heidegger calls the *Mit-sein*. It presupposes my existence, the existence of the *other*, my existence *for* the other, and the existence of the Other *for* me."[10] The suggestion is that by locating the process of deception within the structure of *Mit-sein* as Heidegger does in his discussion of the "They-self" of average everydayness, that human freedom is given short shrift. Instead, Sartre argues that the Other is not a part of my fundamental structure, is not *a priori*, and, importantly, cannot serve as a fundamental explanation of human behavior. Instead, for Sartre it works this way: Lying and self-deception, inaccuracy with regard to the perceptions that one provides 'Others' with, are not situations that happen *to* one nor a state of affairs wherein 'something comes over one.' Instead such phenomena are secondary construct that stems from the subsequent constitution of one as a subject among other subjectivities. The ground of the deception involved in *Mit-sein* is not the corporate, agentless "They-self," but rather bad faith. Here, self-deception is phenomenological, and refers back to what Sartre views as the central of existence—one's being-in-the-world on the basis of nothingness, as noted in the earlier discussion of the ontological proof.

In fact, Sartre argues, the essence of the ability to lie to the Other, is that consciousness has a duality—an existence *for-itself* and an existence for the *Other*. As Sartre puts it, in the lie one uses or exploits the duality between myself and how I appear to the other in order to establish pretense. An ontological capability is at work here. For when viewed from the perspective of a 'pseudo'event or interpretation, the lie enables one to create in the *Other* a version of Reality that is false but it does so only as a contingency. It is, of course, contingent upon the fact that the liar is the sole source of information for the recipient of the lie. Viewed from the perspective of a possible reduction, a lie merely represents one facet of a Reality that presumably can be fulfilled by the adoption of other perspectives on the self-same. *Bad faith* is central to Sartre's argument because in self-deception the ability to exploit the duality noted above wherein one exists both *for-oneself* and for the *Other* does not pertain, since one is transparent to oneself all along. Although it appears that one is hiding something unpleasant from oneself and that the structure of bad faith is the same as the lie to the *Other*, the fact remains that there is not a duality but a single transparency. Something like the conditioning of mass society can lead one to believe, Sartre argues, that certain circumstances can be relieved by engaging in bad faith, but, and this is the essential point for Sartre, one must "sign-off" on instances of bad faith in order to bring it about. Again, it is more accurate to say that bad faith does not come from outside, it is akin to an autoimmune response gone awry but instead of one's body turning one one's self, one's consciousness does.

For Sartre, one is first a being-for-oneself and then one experiences the facticity of the world, its psychological, social, and even political constructions. On this score, as some scholars have noted, one experiences the existence of the 'Other' not as an object, but precisely as a subject, and one capable of effectively viewing one's own self as an object. On this score, it is also worth noting that Sartre, during the course of his critique of Heidegger, makes the following point regarding solipsism, itself a subtext of his critique of mainstream psychology: "That if solipsism is to be overcome, the relation to the other—*being-for-others*—cannot be an element of the ontological structure of the *for-itself*. The existence of others is a *contingent* fact, and being-for-others is a mode of being of the *for-itself* that only arises through concrete encounter with the other. The other cannot be deduced from an *a priori for-itself*."[11] For Sartre there cannot be an *a priori* structure, or substrate, whereby the 'Other' and the individual are coalesced into a unity precisely because of the absolute transcendence of the Other. That said, the experience of the other also involves the experience of the 'Other' as an object. How is this possible? For Sartre, Others exist in two modes: As objects for my consciousness and as subjects when one becomes an object in their life. So Sartre begins by noting the discordance between the absolute transcendence of the 'Other' on the one hand, and the paradoxical objectivity of the 'Other,' on the other: "This woman whom I see coming toward me, this man who is passing by on the street, this beggar whom I hear calling before my window, all are for me *objects*—of that there is no doubt. Thus it is true that at least one of the modalities of the Other's presence to me is *object-ness*."[12] For Sartre 'realism' is phenomenological realism and it is this that distinguishes Sartre's 'realism' from both that of McCulloch's positivist interpretation and the 'realism' of psychology. The precise manner, in which phenomenological realism should be understood, as already noted, necessitates the establishment of the intentionality of consciousness as the point of origin for inquiry. However, this type of realism can be discerned most directly in a specific description Sartre provides of the phenomenology of the 'Other:' This is underscored in his discussion of the phenomenology of *Le Regard*. Sartre's account of *Le Regard* establishes the way in which one is an object for the Other.

Sartre uses "*Le Regard*" to verify his central thesis concerning the intentionality of consciousness—that the basic human condition is one of pure immediacy in the world and that all of the structures of the self, including the nomenclature of the self—the "I", the "Ego", "drives", complexes and so forth, are derived from the basic condition, or the "rupture" in ontology, as Sartre puts it. To put the matter otherwise, phenomenology gives rise to ontology and not the reverse.

Sartre discusses this in the context of his description of what takes place in 'the Look'. For Sartre, there is an initial pre-reflective reduction that takes place in "the Look" that helps establish the point that Husserl, when considering the same issue, had missed regarding the ego. For, we read in Sartre's description of "the Look" that the body as a specific set of attributes is bracketed but instead becomes the body purely of the other. For this reason, Sartre tells us that if we see the eyes actually the look vanishes—it is neutralized in the individuality of the person. In other words, the 'Look' refers to a reality that is prior to the formation of the ego, since the latter is derived from previous moments of the *for-itself*. It could be argued, of course, that this position seems quite close to the position that Husserl advanced in *Cartesian Meditations*. However, as noted at the outset, for Sartre the starting point is the unique status of consciousness as generative of the subject, as well as the by-now familiar Sartrean point of the ontological proof that consciousness rests on nothing other than the object of which it is conscious, or in other words nothing. Husserl's position seems to develop in the direction of history and the life-world, or in other words in the direction of ontology as a community of beings, or the more apt term just noted of the "life-world." In point of fact, the delineation of the *life-world* as a super community of beings is precisely the main point of one of Heidegger's critiques of Husserl. Sartre and Heidegger agree about the importance of being *per se* representing a different type of essence (to use the language of the tradition), their disagreement concerns the nature of being—it is nothingness in the case of Sartre. It is interesting to see that in Sartre's account of "the Look" that the first instance is one that is fundamental, and phenomenological. The encounter with the Other delineates the field of perception. Sartre underscores this point in his discussion of encountering a man in a park, and asks about the reference of the man I see in the park as such. Comparing the man to other objects, Sartre notes this difference, if he were like every other object then he would not have the impact on the landscape that he does but instead the mere sight of the other alters the landscape. In contrast to an object, in which case the object can de defined "by the world," what one experiences in the encounter with the Other is something ontologically different. But there is also this strange duality for I am also aware that I am the other for the other, and so I become aware of another status that I possess. The character of this phenomenon is such that, since each defines the spatial experiences of the world for each, the other cannot experience me as he does any other object any more than I can experience him as such. For Sartre there is something quite radical at work in the encounter with the other: It is direct and it is fundamental even while being such that it is given as a totality and not as parts. As Sartre puts it: "Thus the relation which I call 'being-seen-by-another' far from being merely one of the relations signified by the word, *man*, represents an irreducible fact which cannot be deduced either from the essence of the Other-as-object, or from my being-as-subject." We are in the area here of a primordial *recognition* according to which for Sartre: "In a word, my apprehension of the Other in the world as *probably being* a man refers to my permanent possibility of *being seen by him*; that is, to the permanent possibility that a subject who sees me may be substituted for the object seen by me. Being-seen-by-the-Other is the *truth* of seeing the other." The experience of the Other is a daily one, and the Other is the "one who looks at me." The manifestation of this is the phenomenology of the eyes, for "if I apprehend the look (*Le regard*), I cease to perceive the eyes; they are there, they remain in the field of my perception as pure *presentations*, but do not make an use of them; they are neutralized, put out of play; they are no longer the object of a thesis but remain, as noted, in that state of 'disconnection' in which the world is put by a consciousness practicing the phenomenological reduction prescribed by Husserl." Finally, Sartre adds: "It is never when eyes are looking at you that you can find them beautiful or ugly, that you can remark on their color. The Other's look hides his eyes; he seems to go *in front of them*."[13] When the Other appears suddenly one is made aware of the fact that "all of a sudden I am conscious of myself as escaping myself, not in that I am the foundation of my own nothingness but in that I have my foundation outside myself. I am for myself only as I am a pure reference to the Other."[14] What is at work in *Le regard* is the fact of recognition at a primordial level, in which and through which, the "Other is not an object here and cannot be an object, as we have shown, unless by the same stroke *my* self ceases to be an object-for-the-Other and vanishes."[15] Recognition, and of course, intersubjectivity, are established at the very point of origin of *Mit-sein*. As Sartre puts it: "I grasp the Other's look at the very center of my *act* as the solidification and alienation of my own possibilities. In fear or in anxious or prudent anticipation, I perceive that these possibilities which I *am* and which are the condition of my transcendence are given also to another, given as about to be transcended in turn by his own possibilities. The Other as a look is only that—my transcendence transcended."[16] This pre-reflective and primordial knowledge is of a different sort than conceptual or even rational knowledge and is not only the point of origin for Sartre's phenomenology, but it is also the terminus for his philosophy. That is to say, viewed from the perspective (of a possible rejoinder) of McCulloch's criticism of Sartre's epistemology, it represents a response in that this basic knowledge is a baseline in that, given Sartre's argument, it is the case that Reason cannot be 'naturalized' any further beyond the existential correlate of the *for-itself*. On this interpretation of Sartre's philosophy, the existence of the emotions and being-in-the-world as knowledge, that represents a reply not only to McCulloch's critique regarding pseudo-objects, but to the other versions of 'realism' noted above. If one prefers, one can posit a terminus for Sartre in a realist correlate within the so-called natural world, but this correlate, oddly enough, turns out to be the void or 'nothingness' that informs other elements of the life of the mind. In fact, it also informs the mind's own subsequently derived structures, such as the various modalities of ideology that comprise the subject of many of Sartre's plays and novels.

INTENTIONALITY, REALISM AND THE EMOTIONS

Sartre's approach evinces a strong correspondence with aspects of Husserl's argument for phenomenology. It is important to note that here, especially since the emphasis has been placed on those areas of Sartre's argument where his version of Intentionality diverges from that of Husserl. One area f affinity between the two thinkers is that of the idea of originary perception. For example, Sartre relies on Husserl's concept of 'originary perception' throughout his analysis, though for him it involves existential awareness, and does so in the context of 'bad faith.' In fact, he uses very similar language to that employed by Husserl, and to the same purpose, noting the priority of intentionality which serves as the basis of bad faith. That is to say, it is the original position of consciousness relative to itself, which is the Intentionality of consciousness that prevents consciousness from slipping into its own illusions. Furthermore, for Sartre, the whole edifice of deception including the establishment of the pseudo-objects is based on bad faith. One needs precisely to know the truth to be an effective liar to oneself.

However, because bad faith is grounded in the Intentionality of consciousness amounts to a negative form of phenomenological or existential freedom. For that reason, even f one wished to escape the awareness of bad faith, there is still a residue that is traceable to one's existential freedom and that retains an awareness that one is in bad faith. In sum, even if one wished to lie to oneself, the lie, in effect is destroyed from behind, so to speak, by the Intentionality of consciousness itself. Conversely, it is of course also the case that bad faith is something that one can live with, even as a normal feature of daily existence. Nevertheless, its presence within the life of the mind is precarious, Sartre argues, and can be dissolved at any instance. Indeed, one can be attached to expressions of bad faith, which when dislodged, give rise to a certain bewilderment owing both to one's inability to comprehend, on the one hand, or reject outright on the other, the existence of bad faith as something present to one all along.

The point that Sartre makes regarding bad faith is, to a certain extent, similar to Sartre's critique of Husserl. It concerns realism, for, just as we saw in his critique of Husserl that Sartre accepted some key Husserlian ideas, and reserved his criticisms primarily for the fact that Husserl failed to extend his analysis of intentionality to the ego itself, and that, in a word it was not radical enough; so too, with regard to Freud, it is not that Sartre criticizes Freud for his radicalism, but that he too failed to extend the revolutionary and radical nature of his ideas to their most radical conclusion.

We have already introduced Sartre's account of Freud's idea of repression, what seems useful at this juncture is to elaborate further on this "debate" from the perspective of bad faith. Our purpose in doing so is two-fold. First, we want to underscore the radicalism of Sartre's Realism. Secondly, we want to also highlight the relationship between Realism and freedom. At the end of the day there is a symmetry between Sartre's doctrine of Realism and his account of freedom. The consideration of Freud and psychology generally, affords us the opportunity to approach this issue from the perspective of the psychic life of the individual.

For Sartre, the kind of first or initial awareness that one experiences is that of being-in-the-world. It is, in fact, of a piece with Sartre's Realism. We saw earlier, and have stressed throughout, that this duality is basic and definitive of human existence. But psychoanalysis also presents a duality, and indeed, the self is bifurcated, Sartre argues, but it is not mediated therein by a censor. The bifurcation is that which exists between the for-itself and the in-itself is used by psychoanalysis to posit the duality of the conscious and the unconscious under the guidance of the censor. Psychoanalysis, and by extension other psychological methodologies that have recourse to repression merely replaces the bi-frication of consciousness with a duality at the level of the censor.

The structures that Sartre introduces in the course of his delineation of consciousness—being-for-others and being-for-itself—enable him to incorporate the emotions into his Realism as entities that are as real as the objects with which they come to be associated. The emotions are 'real' and are not parasitic upon real events since they themselves are factual and are not merely or even primarily symbolic. The message that Sartre intends to underscore in all of this is nothing less than the idea that the true source of neurosis is not the repression of drives, or complexes, but the initial event of which these are later theoretical instantiations—*bad faith itself*, which is a disruption of being-in-the-world. Thus, psychoanalysis is an instantiation of a double phenomenon of *bad faith*, in that, on the one hand the patient is encouraged to believe in the existence of this hidden Reality, and on the other, that the practitioner, to the extent that he or she makes uses of this construct, also engages in a theoretical reification of *bad faith*. In place of this, Sartre argues for the primacy of existential realism, or phenomenology. As he puts it: "Proponents of the theory have hypostasized and 'reified' *bad faith*; they have not escaped it."[17]

For Sartre, a chief difficulty with psychoanalysis is that it represents an attempt to move from a realist perspective to one which is ideological and that is conducted through the symbolic interpretation of experience. Thus, the idea of reified consciousness, which, as noted above is the primary charge that Sartre levels against psychoanalysis, involves assessing the extent to which realism in the case of psychic life refers to actual events and not symbolic constructions. For Sartre, the actual event of hiding and subsequently creating additional constructs is precisely the meaning of *bad faith*. Of course, it should be noted in this context, that one of the most persistent of contemporary criticisms of Freud concerns his revision of his own realism– a critique that surfaces most acutely perhaps in his revision of the seduction-abandonment thesis.

In the case of Sartre's Realism there is an additional element that needs to be accounted for and that is the relationship that exists between his Realism and his approach to temporality. Again, this is something that is brought into relief in comparison with, or in juxtaposition with, his critique of Freudian psychoanalysis. For Freud and for psychoanalysis generally, attempts at Realism involve the reassembly of actual events, their possible reconstruction as sublimated or transferred phenomenon, and their eventual delineation under the tutelage of the therapist. It is, in essence, a relationship that is guided by a discourse, on several levels, between the past and the present. However, for Sartre, given his conception of the Intentionality of consciousness, the temporality of psychoanalysis is itself problematic. This is due only in part to the central place of the future in Sartre's philosophy. We emphasize only because the temporality of Sartre's philosophy is informed throughout by the Intentionality of consciousness. It is this fact that gives weight to the primacy of the future. The intentionality of consciousness requires first of all the fact that consciousness is recognized as being unable to concretize itself as a in-itself, in the first instance, a phenomenon that is traceable to the ground of consciousness in a "lack."

There is a sense in which Sartre's analysis of psychoanalysis evinces a different approach to temporality in that for Sartre, even if one decides to examine one's past, under the guidance of a therapist, including those of the recent past of an hour ago, one is, for Sartre, always doing so by way of a basic directedness towards the future. One *puts the past before one*. The intentionality of consciousness, in this context, means that interpretations are not fixed in the past, but instead, emerge from the future horizon of the intentionality of consciousness. As Mazis puts it: "Through these disturbances, these gaps in intention, new meanings emerge which form themselves into new significations that transform the possibilities of the person to whom they are manifest."[18] An important part of existential freedom is the idea that one's idea, or concept of one's self is not fixed, of course, but this is true both with regard to both thought and *praxis*. That is to say, one can think of themselves as other than they currently are, but one can also bring that about through one's own *praxis*, which is also radically open towards the future.

As we saw, Sartre's critique of traditional psychoanalysis on the basis of temporality also involves setting consciousness apart as first, being-in-the-world and radically open to the future. By virtue of its Intentionality, consciousness is capable, in Sartre's view, of establishing constructs such as the ego in order to avoid the delineation, if not the awareness, of 'nothingness' as a point of origin. It is worth recalling the passage cited by Mazis from *The Transcendence of the Ego* to make this point: "But perhaps the essential role of the ego is to mask from consciousness its very spontaneity. A phenomenological description of spontaneity would show, indeed, that spontaneity renders impossible any distinction between action and passion, or any conception of an autonomy of the will."[19]

To sum up this aspect of Sartre's critique of traditional psychoanalysis, the dialogue between consciousness as in-itself and consciousness as for-itself implies the centrality of the future. Sartre adds this core criticism to his rejection of other Freudian structures—the structure of the id, ego, and superego. This also, of course, includes the idea of repression, and the complexes themselves as unacknowledged, unknown sources of action, culminating in the privileging of sexuality over other emotions such as love.

In place of the archaeology of Freud, in which case there is a residue from the past that above all else must be excavated; an alternative view is the one introduced by Adler. He introduces a temporal horizon, or a geographical landscape defined at one end by the child's sense of inferiority in the face of adults—parents, relatives and others—and the position occupied at the adult end—wherein the individual escapes from this state of affairs by effecting a superior stance. However, the struggle to overcome this initial inferiority is the core of Adler's study (Stern, 1967).

Some analyses of Sartre and Adler argue that the latter is not only compatible with Sartre's account of consciousness, but that Adler anticipated Sartre's analysis (Stern, 1967). One can, of course, argue that there are some superficial similarities here, but these similarities aside; there are so many significant differences between existential psychoanalysis generally (including the role of the intentionality of consciousness) that the comparison appears to be overdrawn. For, the differences between Adler and Sartre evince radically conflicting visions of the philosophy of mind, the philosophy of time, the earlier noted uniqueness of existential freedom, and perhaps most significant of all, Sartre's phenomenological account of realism. For Adler, there is most definitely a discernable human essence. It has been alluded to throughout this analysis, and now it should be said most directly, that Sartre's account of Intentionality is of far greater significance than the often touted existential heroism of the individual. The project of overcoming early childhood inferiority, while certainly a powerful way of presenting human development, is not as fundamental a feature of human existence as is the bifurcation of consciousness, its grounding in a "lack" and the uniqueness of existential freedom.

We have been studying the relationship between Sartre and psychology generally, Freud and Adler specifically, because Sartre's emphasis on existential freedom implies negation, including a more complete negation of those elements of the socialization process that are destructive, both to the individual and the community. In the main, the emphasis within psychoanalysis is on the study of the repression of biological drives and the initiation of fundamental complexes. However, on Sartre's account the psychological effects of alienation are more discernable and increasingly susceptible to critique from Sartre's. This is because it stresses the <u>total</u> freedom of the individual as coeval with the most basic structure of Reality: the Intentionality of consciousness as bifurcated and as being-in-the-world.

The primary difficulty that surfaces in comparing Sartre's phenomenological account of Reality with that for most psychological accounts is the one noted earlier by Gurwitsch. He noted that the phenomenological fact of consciousness as a being-in-the-world implies that the delineation of consciousness is not accurately pursued from that of empirical psychology. This is primarily because of its reliance on an ontology of the "I." Proceeding from empirical ontology, the ontic, to the most fundamental fact of human existence, has the effect of obscuring a more basic point that Sartre's philosophy attempts to address. Thus, for example, while one can speak of freedom in various ways, in ways that accommodate the ontology of Adler it remains the case that for Sartre's philosophy 'freedom' represents a primordial starting point that is thoroughly phenomenological, involving the dichotomy, once again, between consciousness as *in-itself* and as *for-itself.*

NOTES

1. Glen A. Mazis, "A New Approach to Sartre's Theory of the Emotions," in Existential Ontology and Human Consciousness, ed. William McBride (New York: Garland Publishing, 1997): 130.

2. Ibid.: 130.

3. Sartre, op. cit., 1966: 57

4. Ibid.:61.

5. Another important question is the relationship between Freud's concept of the *libido* and Sartre's description of consciousness. Some scholars have viewed Freud as a phenomenologist and his concept of *libido* radically non-essentialist.

6. Sartre, op. cit., 1966:62.

7. Ibid.: 64.

8. Ibid.: 59.

9. It is also, of course, one of the elements that distinguishes Sartre's existential philosophy from other systems of thought that emphasize the individual and 'objective reality.' Here one thinks of the writings of Ayn Rand, whose writings certainly emphasize the individual and the objective order, but whose philosophy is totally devoid of both intersubjectivity and ontology, two key elements at work in Sartre's existentialism.

10. Ibid.: 58.

11. Ibid.

12. Ibid.: 310.

13. Ibid.: 315-317.

14. Ibid.: 319.

15. Sartre depicted this aspect of the Other famously in his play No Exit, but the conspicuous absence of mirrors.

16. Ibid.: 322.

17. Ibid.: 65.

18. Mazis, op. cit., : 130.

19. Ibid.: 128.

Chapter Five

Political Theory and Alienation

Thus far we have considered the ground of freedom in Sartre's philosophy and its relationship to Intentionality. One of the core issues has been that if Sartre's theory of intentionality is true then one of the essential components of the new essentialism must be wrong. Our next step will be to elucidate how this develops into a theory of alienation, or to be more precise, political alienation that establishes history and not genetics as the most appropriate point of origin for human destruction both at the individual and social level. We are dealing here no longer with the foundation of human freedom but with the reified categories that have sprung up and that are used to abstractly depict the politics of scarcity.

In this section of our work we will limit our analysis to a consideration of Sartre's early theory of alienation as a critique of the ideology of essentialism. We will begin by setting the context for Sartre's theory of alienation, and by extension, politics. It may be useful to begin our analysis by recalling that long before his estrangement from Camus and later, Merleau-Ponty, over the relationship between authenticity and political commitment, Sartre had a clear idea about the relationship that exists between ideology, including political ideology, and existential freedom. For Sartre, politics is built into the very fabric of Reality. This is, of course, an idea that surfaces in his early novels and plays, as well as in his depiction of bad faith. On this score, one idea that we want to explicate in this portion of our analysis is that of the threefold relationship among freedom, Realism, and politics in Sartre's early works. The point that will be advanced here is that for Sartre existence is a political category. As noted, this is apparent in many of his early works. We have already introduced some key ideas from his early novel, *Nausea*. Here we will continue to examine the foundations of ideology but from the vantage point of Sartre's philosophical writings, especially in comparison to Martin Heidegger. The procedure we will follow then is as follows: First, we will re-iterate the key elements of Sartre's theory of Intentionality from the early philosophical works, and then in the following chapter we will use this to ex-plicate Sartre's early theory of social evil in his play, *The Flies.*

Sartre's theory of alienation appears for the first time in his early work on "Intentionality" and in his study *The Transcendence of the Ego.* Both of these texts have already been explicated in the first two sections of this analysis. Throughout these works, we have been stressing the fact that for Sartre the point of origin for an accurate assessment of Reality is that of the bifurcation of consciousness. However, what we want to accomplish as part of our analy-sis here is to locate this axiomatic position within the context of the Western study of alienation, especially as a political phenomenon. For example, we want to pose the question: Where does Sartre fit in that tradition?

In terms of locating Sartre's theory of alienation and politics in the history of Western thought, Sartre represents a critique of a de-ontological approach to politics, or an ontology that is *from* being. For, what Sartre is arguing for is the priority of Intentionality as coeval with freedom. One can see this if one compares Sartre's concept of freedom with the liberal conception of freedom in the tradition from Hobbes, Locke, and Mill. It may be useful, by way of providing an illustration, to note this briefly before proceeding.

We should begin in the modern era, with Hobbes, who, as the foundational figure for liberal political philosophy is quite clear about the fact that the on-tology of the self is of little or no concern to political philosophy. We can see this in his treatment of the foundation of ethics and human agency when, in *Leviathan* Hobbes argues that men are equal in that each one has the capac-ity to kill the other. After making this point, Hobbes basically asks his reader, then what? What follows in the pages of Leviathan is a careful articulation of the consequences of this stated fact. Other thinkers in the liberal democratic tradition, such as Mill refine the arguments of liberalism of course, but the ba-sic premise of liberalism is de-ontic. It is true, of course, that in the case of John Stuart Mill there is the additional element of *utilitarianism,* and the in-troduction of the *harm principle.* However, the basic liberal premise of liber-alism establishes that the fundamental question of human agency may simply be posited and that references to ontology *per se* should be bracketed. The difficulty with this position is the one that has, in recent times, been the focus of analysis by *critical theorists:* The idea that liberal political philosophy is not critical enough about what it presupposes regarding the point of origin for analysis. For Sartre, ontology does matter, and it is in this context that Sartre's theory of alienation is best understood. The way in which the Other is en-countered, as a free and total existence, means that the phenomenon of recognition, for example, is not merely to be considered as part of the social contract. Instead, on Sartre's reading, it is more accurately depicted as referring to a prior moment of Reality. For, just as bad faith involves a more primary relationship to the Reality of one's self, so too recognition of the Other is a component of sincerity. At the same time however, it is also important to recall an earlier point that was made regarding *Mit-sein* during the course of our analysis of "the Look." There, it will be recalled that we made the point that what the discussion of "the Look" underscores is that *Mit-sein* is not to be conceived of as an *a priori* structure of the self. Otherwise, as Sartre points out, the Other's subjectivity would be an extension of my being, and thus, involve a fairly severe undermining of freedom and agency. Instead, the Other, by virtue of the fact that the Other is just that, a complete and total subjectivity, who by their mere presence and "Look" can limit me as a free agent and objectify me. The nuance here is that while *Mit-sein* is not prior to consciousness, or an *a priori* structure of consciousness, the layered effect of which leads to the subsequent constitution of the subject. It follows then that, since the "I" is derived from the more primary phenomenology: Being-in-the-world as the Intentionality of consciousness, the Western tradition tends to discount ontology, even while it emphasizes behavior, as we saw above in our discussion of Hobbes.

So, from a Sartrean point of view the positing of "I" as the starting point for an inquiry into the basis for politics, reflects the problems he depicted in his overall critique of subjectivity: the failure of the tradition to give priority to consciousness, the trivializing of the imagination and the emotions, and a latent de-emphasis on ontology, one result of which is a strong de-ontological tradition. One reason for this, of course, is that for Sartre it is only after the Intentionally of consciousness that the "I" of the tradition appears. In other words, by shifting his focus in this way and making consciousness synonymous with the world, wherein, again, conscious rests on nothing more than the object of which it is conscious, the search for an initial political foundation must always be derivative of the Intentionality of consciousness.

The question that is usually posed at this point, where we are tracing Sartre's political philosophy is this: How is it possible for Sartre to argue that the radical freedom of the individual, developed as it is on the basis of Sartre's theory of Intentionality, in which and through which consciousness is bifurcated, and in such a way that the "I" is subsequent to consciousness, is neither ideological, nor essentialist? The answer, by this time a familiar one, involves recalling that for Sartre the ground of consciousness itself is a "lack." So, it is not a question of essential structures at all, but rather of alienation. It just so happens that the reason that Sartre's concept of freedom is itself immune from the charge of ideology and reification is that both constructs are derivative of a more basic relationship of consciousness to the world. The layering effect that Sartre depicts in his philosophy, especially in *Being and Nothingness* concerns the role of *Mit-sein*. The question is: How does Sartre supports this position?

Sartre uses the example of what goes on during the experience of shame to underscore his position regarding *Mit-sein,* and to distinguish it from that of Heidegger. Shame is also an instance that may be used to deconstruct the essentialist view that somehow some people, presumably those with a genetic predisposition, are more prone to experience shame than others. Instead, Sartre argues that shame is thoroughly existential and a reflection of the primordial state he defines as being-in-the-world. One can discover one's self, of course, in certain circumstances such as shame, and what one discovers is that one's consciousness "sticks" to one's acts, wherein, moreover, "it *is* my acts; and my acts are commanded only by the ends to be attained and by the instruments to be employed." It is in such circumstances that: "The order is the reverse of the causal order. It is the end to be attained which organizes all the moments which precede it."[1] The transversals of Intentionality are now reorganized on the basis of the experience of the Other. I am recognized by the Other, of course, but now that moment of recognition is part of my existence: In shame, one is compelled to recognize one's self.

What Sartre is arguing for in this passage is the idea that the freedom of the individual is inextricably intertwined with the Intentionality of consciousness according to which the constitution of the 'subject' is developed subsequently. For, a few passages later we read that one 'discovers' one's ego in the experience of shame: "Nevertheless, I am that Ego; I do not reject it as a strange image, but it is present to me as a self which I am without *knowing* it; for I discover it in shame and, in other instances, in pride. It is shame and pride which reveals to me the Other's look and myself at the end of that look. It is shame or pride which make me *live*, not know the situation of being looked at."[2] For Sartre, one lives ethics first. There is an extraordinary set of consequences for this intersection of politics and ethics. For it entails that anti-Semitism or racism exist at the level of recognition, the level of *Le regard*. What we are considering here is the very ground of human intersubjectivity. For, Sartre asks us to consider the implicit self-knowledge that one experiences in shame. We know we are what we are even though through bad faith we might try to hide that from ourselves. However, bad faith is nothing so much as a confirmation of the basic self-knowledge one has from being-in-the-world and transparent to one's self. For, bad faith is, as noted earlier, tantamount to a negative argument for the freedom of consciousness. Sartre then notes that this type of existential recognition is a possibility on the basis of this primordial freedom: "Thus each of my free conducts engages me in a new environment where the very stuff of my being is the unpredictable freedom of another. Yet, by my very shame I claim as mine that freedom of another. I affirm a profound unity of consciousness, not that harmony of monads which has sometimes been taken as a guarantee of objectivity but a unity of being; for I accept and wish that others should confer upon me a being which I recognize."[3]

The answer to the question then, of how Sartre grounds a philosophy of freedom that is neither itself ideological nor essentialist is that the Intentionality of consciousness involves a very specific form of intersubjectivity. It is one that is involves being-in-the-world and thereby also involves, as being-in-the-world both subjectivity and objectivity. Finally, it is also one where the Other is a full independent consciousness that is not a part of an *a priori* structure of the self. For, by the same token, one "encounters" the Other as we saw in the discussion of "the Look," primarily because as prior to the subject, it is also prior to ideology or essence.

For Sartre, freedom is best described as a pure description of the structure of consciousness. Along these lines, freedom refers less to the traditional formulations: The absence of external impediments; 'positive' and 'negative' freedom; teleological freedom (in which one actualizes their essence); or even volitional freedom. Instead, for Sartre, all of these formulations have as their basis a more foundational freedom: That of consciousness as a "lack." Grounded in the Intentionality of consciousness itself, freedom for Sartre is the necessary condition that results when consciousness is expelled into the world as transcendence.[4] Once again, the idea of this necessary freedom is captured in his depiction of the Intentionality of consciousness as being-in-the-world. Thus, we return to the key early text, the article on Intentionality where Sartre establishes the relationship between ontology and epistemology, or that there is a kind of self-knowledge implicit in existence as such.

One political consequence of Sartre's depiction of freedom involves a politics of Realism. It is, in effect, a vantage point of a bi-furcated consciousness: Its epistemological element and its phenomenology are united in a single phenomenology of consciousness. The radicalism of Sartre's approach here, and arguably a considerable amount of the power of his argument, comes from the fact that *Mit-sein* is not depicted by him, as noted, as an *a priori* structure of the self. In order to underscore the significance of Sartre's contribution here, it may be useful to contrast it with that of Heidegger, his main adversary on this topic. Secondarily, there is a general feeling within political thought that Heidegger's depiction is stronger and has more to offer as a critique of ideology. On this issue at least, we would like to introduce some contrary evidence.

It will be recalled that in *Being and Time* Heidegger had argued that one of the ways of *Dasein's* being is that of average everydayness. Furthermore, one sees that within this context that *Dasein* has a corporate existence, an existence that Heidegger terms the *they-self.* Heidegger further maintains that *Dasein* "belongs" to the "they-self" enhance its power, and that when one asks the question as to how it is that things come about in this mode of being, that it is without agency. Heidegger is quite explicit on this issue. So, one question that arises, especially in the context of using Heidegger's analysis for the purposes of grounding political philosophy, is how it is that one can act politically when so much about human agency is doubt.

It seems that by reading Heidegger through Sartre, that the difficulty here involves the scope of human agency. Are they categories that are coeval with human freedom and being-in-the-world? In a word, for Sartre they are and for Heidegger, they are not. In the case of the latter, this owes to the problem of the *they-self of average everydayness.*

In fact, Sartre avoids this problem by virtue of the way he establishes the relationship between Intentionality and Realism. For, Sartre takes a position exactly contrary to the one advanced by Heidegger. Again, it will be recalled that the problem of authenticity involves the posing of the following question: How does one act authentically when for the most part one is enmeshed in the *they-self,* or, if one prefers, alienated? It is addressed by Heidegger by proposing a positive role for death. "Being-towards-death" becomes the means by which *Dasein* hears the "call of conscience" and possibly becomes an authentic actor.[5]

Sartre will have none of this and rejects this entire formulation, including that of assigning a positive role for human mortality. Instead, Sartre takes the view that it is the experience of one's self as a "lack" that compels one to acknowledge both their existential freedom and their responsibility.[6]

It is telling that Heidegger admits to the flaw in his argument in his correspondence to Sartre. On this score, Safranski, in his study of Heidegger reproduces a letter from Heidegger that was discovered by Hugo Ott. In the letter Heidegger credits Sartre for a breakthrough in thinking through the problems posed by phenomenology and he specifically acknowledges that Sartre had the better perspective on death. For Sartre had objected that Heidegger's idea of projecting oneself toward death covered up the scandal of death, its absurdity and absolute contingency. It played no positive role in human life as Heidegger argued.

Here we begin to see the full ramifications of this 'oversight' in terms of the consequences for political philosophy. The problem is that for Heidegger, "Being-with-others" is either an inauthentic category, since it is of secondary importance to moods and being-towards-death; or it is neutral. A major problem then concerns assessing just how it is that one overcomes this type of alienation.[7]

THE ISSUE OF *MIT-SEIN* AND SEXUALITY

Sartre argues that there is an additional difficulty regarding the status of *Mit-sein* in Heidegger's philosophy and it is that of sexuality. Sartre critically underscores this point in his analysis during which he notes that being-for-others needs to be considered as being radically intersubjective. Because the subject is famously foreclosed by Heidegger, both because of his version of phenomenology and because of the status of *Dasein* itself as not being of intrinsic interest to Heidegger's study, there are limitations for using his analysis for the study of the body generally, and the politics of sexual identity specifically. Yet, arguably, both of these areas are of great significance for contemporary political thought. But what does Sartre have to say about this especially in the context of *Mit-sein*? Because consciousness is the focus of Sartre's approach, he too avoids the overemphasis on "subjectivity" that Heidegger viewed as problematic, but, for the self-same reason, that of the centrality of the Intentionality of consciousness, Sartre is able to posit a role for intersubjectivity and the body.

One illustration of the difference regarding *Mit-sein* in Heidegger and Sartre involves, as noted Sartre's discussion of sexuality. As he puts it: ". . . This is why existential philosophies have not believed it necessary to concern themselves with sexuality. Heidegger, in particular, does not make the slightest allusion to it in his existential analytic with the result that his 'Dasein' appears to us as asexual. Of course, one may consider that it is contingent for 'human reality' to be specified as 'masculine' or 'feminine' of course one may say that the problem of sexual differentiation has nothing to do with that of *Existnce (Existenz)* since man and woman equally exist. . . . Can we admit that this tremendous matter of the sexual life comes as a kind of addition to the human condition? Yet it appears at first glance that desire and its opposite, sexual repulsion, are fundamental structures of being-for-others. . . Man, it is said, is a sexual being because he possesses a sex. And if the reverse were true? If sex were only the instrument and, so to speak, the *image* of a fundamental sexuality? If man possessed a sex only because he is originally and fundamentally a sexual being as a being who exists in the world in relation with other men?"[8] Just as we saw with the issue of shame, for Sartre, sexuality is not a human essence, still less a category that defines us. The famous statement by de Beauvoir that a woman is made not born is fully consistent with Sartre's concept of intentionality. But what of sexual identity itself? Isn't that an essential category of human existence and doesn't it all but define us as human beings? Some of the confusion here stems from the misnomer according to which Sartre is arguing that one "chooses" their sexuality. This is but a continuation of the misreading of Sartre's philosophy as one that advocates a "freedom of the will." He lampooned this idea and took pains to point out that the kind of freedom he is talking about is the freedom of intentionality, of being-in-the-world and of direct realism. It is not, to reiterate, freedom of the will. So it is not a matter of choosing one's sexuality at all, as though this were a choice like all others, but rather a matter of existential openness towards various sexual subjectivities which for Sartre also always presupposed by a more basic state—that of being-in-the-world. We should now return to the explication of the relationship between the individual and the Other including the community that results from Sartre's account of *Mit-sein*.

We have been considering the radicalism of Sartre's doctrine of *Mit-sein* and arguing that, especially in comparison to Heidegger that Sartre's approach to the question seems to be stronger. This is not to say that other aspects of Heidegger's argument have these limitations, but, since our concern here is politics, that with respect to the efficacy of political theory, the issue of *Mit-sein* appears to us to be highly relevant. For Sartre, human agency is the unavoidable fate that comes to one at birth as a result of the intentional structure of consciousness. For example, in *Being and Nothingness* Sartre turns his attention to the structure of consciousness within the context of transcendence. In place of the language of the whirlwind in the essay on phenomenology, in this later work Sartre employs more epistemological language to note the disparity between the *for-itself* and the *in-itself*. As he puts it: "If I conceive of a being entirely closed in on itself, this being in itself will be solely that which it is, and due to this fact there will be no room for either negation or knowledge."[9] Following up on this point Sartre emphasizes that that there is an ethical component to Intentionality along with agency. On this score, there is a close affinity between Intentionality and ethics in both Sartre and Husserl is a feature of their respective concepts of Intentionality, which both include human agency.[10] In terms of political theory then, one may say that for Sartre political ethics is grounded in the relationship, a logically necessary one, between Intentionality and agency.

Negation is an expression of this agency, for Sartre tells us that: "In short, the term-of-origin of the internal negation is the *in-itself*, the thing which *is there*, and outside of it there is nothing except an emptiness, a nothingness which is distinguished from the thing only by a pure negation for which *this* thing furnishes the very content."[11] Negating is a key element since it expresses the relationship between freedom and realism, on the one hand, and agency and ethics, on the other. This is an important point for political theory, especially with regard to the experience of ideology, for negation serves the function of choosing between bad faith and sincerity.

The emphasis on nothing and negation is also important because it establishes the parameters for Sartre's political argument, or the application of the same: The idea that outside of the fact of human freedom there is simply no additional idea or structure that can lay claim to being an essence. It follows, *ipso facto* that all other perceived structures and alleged essences may be explicated, or in some instances, critiqued, without the possibility of reifying the categories of analysis, including political analyses. Again, for Sartre, "There is nothing outside the *in-itself* except a reflection of that nothing which is itself polarized (the *for-itself* among the plenitude of being), and defined by the *in-itself* inasmuch as it is precisely the nothingness of *this* in-itself, the individualized nothing which is nothing only because it is not the *in-itself*."[12] The difficulty that Sartre sees here involves not just an epistemological point, but an ontological one. It is, for him, a mistake to believe that one can start with things and then derive consciousness. For Sartre it is more valid to begin with a realist position, and then to ask: How is it possible to have ideas about things in the world from a realist perspective. Furthermore, it is also a mistake, in Sartre's view, to understand Being *per se* as a phenomenon that can be explained *via* the plenitude of beings, or entitativly.

For Sartre, starting with the realist position is itself an expression of politics. Sartre criticizes a certain form of realism best described by Kosik as the *pseudo concrete* (Kosik, 1976). The point here is that, just as the idealist position can express reified categories of analysis,[13] so too there is a type of reified realist position can be discerned in a form of materialism that devolves to an infinite regress by appealing to ever new formulations of materialism in order to totalize the human condition. The duality of consciousness means that the individual can transcend his situation, since one consequence of existential freedom, (itself ultimately grounded in the structure of consciousness as intentionality), is a mandate that even the 'situation' give way to the more significant role of consciousness. As Hazel Barnes notes on this score: "Sartre never denies the existence of conditions, but he insists (as Marx did) that it is still men who *make* the history. This is because the most fundamental characteristic of man as consciousness is his ability to go beyond his situation."[14]

We see this point illustrated in Sartre's play *The Flies*, where Orestes, by virtue of his existence, represents a threat to both god and King. This is his situation, and his existence itself brings him into conflict with the bad faith of the citizens of Argos, and that of political authority. It is important to note that the opposition that Sartre describes is pre-discursive, existing the level of ontology. More will be said about this shortly, the point here is that there is a three-fold political expression of Sartre's concept of Intentionality: Freedom, intersubjectivity, and realism. As noted at the outset of our analysis, these operate as a baseline for one's being-in-the-world. Implied here is a kind of politics that may be described as inter-subjective, except that for Sartre, the Intentionality of consciousness is prior to the subject.

The situated individual, as contextualized by freedom, intersubjectivity and Reality, is depicted by Sartre in his political analysis and surfaces most directly in his narrative works, where it functions as the basis of the critique of ideology and received ideas. The Wall, The Flies, The Condemned of Altona and even longer works such as his trilogy, The Age of Reason, are all illustrations of the extent to which the Intentionality of consciousness was used by Sartre to undermine a cacophony of received ideas and ideologies. A distinction should be made here between the kind of politics we are describing, the immediacy of Intentionality, and the second-order politics that surfaces in some of Sartre's other political writings and articles. The latter often evince the idea of commitment, a mainstay of Sartre's engagement in politics, including the politics of theorizing and political journalism. Here we want to note that while the idea of politics as commitment was certainly an important one for Sartre, nevertheless it is not the most fundamental meaning of politics in Sartre's philosophy. Instead, the concept of politics we are addressing here is much closer to the ancient political concept of politics as *strife*.[15] This is a concept of politics that has recurred throughout the history of Western political philosophy, although Sartre's way of depicting it by way of phenomenology is unique. Also, because of the Sartrean emphasis on agency, it differs markedly from the kind of political philosophy that one can cull from Heidegger's depiction of fundamental ontology. On this score, it is interesting to note that the first expression of the idea of politics as a first principle was that of the *Anaximander Fragment*, which most scholars view as a fundamental text for approaching the Presocratic idea of politics. It was also, of course, used by Heidegger to explicate his own philosophy. Here, the idea that is conveyed by the Presocratic philosophers was a concept of justice in which strife and justice are dialectical. This is especially true of Heraclitus as Hegel's analysis underscored in his study of the topic. "Strife" itself is also a major motif of Solon in writings attributed to him, and it also surfaces in the writings of Empedocles. The general idea is that a penalty is entailed for violating a primordial balance, be it excessive attention to the ego, at the level of the individual, or excessive social imbalance in which the penalty is non-being, or annihilation.[16] Of concern to us here, is not the precise interpretation of the idea of *strife*, but rather, the fact that it was and is an idea that has been a continuing theme in the Western tradition of political philosophy.

However, for the most part, other than to say that the human condition is defined by *strife*, political philosophy has generally avoided the question of *how* and *why* that is the case.[17] The earlier noted approach taken by Thomas Hobbes illustrates the tendency among political philosophers to note it as a fact and then to move on to questions such as political obligation and rights. However, it is important to note that for the early Greek thinkers the question of "why" or "how" strife was a first principle was considered beyond Reason. This assessment, of course, is continued in the modern era in Political Philosophy within the liberal tradition. Sartre's concept of Intentionality is an exception. For, in terms of political thought Sartre's concept on intentionality marks a retrun to an ontological approach to political theory. In other words, his theory of consciousness accounts *strife* at the level of ontology, or being-in-the-world. It is a first principle of his philosophy as we saw in the account of recognition he advanced and is also underscored in his account of scarcity, the topic of our last chapter in this study. Another way of saying this is to note that Sartre's doctrine of the Intentionality of consciousness makes reintroduces existence as such as a political category. We can see this argument advanced in Sartre's early play *The Flies*, and so, an explication of that play from the vantage point of the ground of politics can serve two purposes. It can, as noted, underscore by way of exposition what Sartre has to say about politics. Secondly, it can also place that contribution in the context of the origin of Western thinking about politics.On this score, specifically, Sartre's analysis underscores the tension between secular and religious authority on the one hand, and the individual, on the other. Of course, this was an emphasis that Aeschylus himself contributed to. The emphasis in Sartre's account, however, is on the citizens of Argos, and the phenomenon of bad faith, as a kind of plague that one afflicts one's self with.[18] For Sartre the experience of the politics of alienation seems to have at its core a fundamental aspect of being-in-the-world. The everyday experiences of alienation, or its accumulated evidence in mass behavior, statistical research, and what is generally referred to as *negativities*, seem to presuppose a more fundamental alienation that, Sartre argues, is directly related to the Intentionality of consciousness. For, one could say that just as bad faith can serve as a foundation for the individual's susceptibility and acquiescence to systematic social control and propaganda, so too, this fundamental state of politics can serve as a template for reifying religious and traditional authority, on the one hand, and the explicitly political form of authority exercised by the state, on the other. *The Flies* provides an illustration of this non-recognition that is coeval with bad faith, having as its basis, the Intentionality of consciousness. We can see this point a bit more clearly if we consider the issue of obligation.

The idea of obligation is part of a continuing political discourse not just between philosophers of social contract theory, such as Hobbes and Rousseau, but more recently, between communitarians and libertarians. Of course, both sides of this debate frequently invoke the idea of individual responsibility for one's acts as a preface to their discussions, and in fact, the discourse of obligation as responsibility has become a mainstay of conservative and liberal, as well as neo-liberal social philosophy. The Sartrean account of obligation and responsibility is a departure from these accounts and focusing on obligation and responsibility allows the analysis to thematize Sartre's theory of alienation. We should begin by considering how Sartre presents the issue of responsibility in *The Flies*. The citizens of Argos, we are told, have been afflicted with a plague and it is one that is marked by the appearance of huge flies soon after the murder of Agamemnon by Aigisthus and Clytemnestra. However, Sartre reverses the causal order and maintains that bad faith is such that it leads the citizens to posit the effect, the murder of Agamemnon, as the cause. In fact, the cause of the plague is bad faith. To put the matter somewhat differently, it is ontology that gives rise to social pathologies. 'Responsibility' in this sense then, refers to a prior phenomenological fact, and that fact is the fact of recognition. It is, in the case of Sartre, a recognition that is immediate, direct, and can be either positive as recognition, or a negative stance towards one's self or the Other: "My consciousness is not restricted *envisioning a negatite*, it constitutes itself in its own flesh as the nihilation of a possibility which another human reality projects as its possibility."[19] Sartre elaborates on the fundamental state of this negation further in his analysis of the phenomenology of "the Look." He notes the foundation aspect of this: "Thus, the relation which I call 'being-seen-by-another,' far from being merely one of the relations signified by the word *man*, represents an irreducible fact which can not be deduced either from the essence of the Other-as-object, or from my being-as-subject"[20] To underscore this point, Sartre introduces the *situation* of what happens when one is suddenly 'discovered' at a keyhole spying on another. In the course of describing this state of affairs, and to understand the radical effect that the recognition or negation that the 'Other' represents, Sartre describes the consciousness as *non-thetic*. "I am alone," Sartre tells us, "and on the level of a non-thetic self-consciousness. This means first of all that there is no self to inhibit my consciousness, nothing therefore to which I can refer my acts in order to qualify them. They are in no way known; I am my acts and hence they carry in themselves their whole justification."[21] In this passage, Sartre is also introducing the concept of the *situation*, which will figure prominently in his later works of political philosophy. By positing the idea of non-thetic consciousness, wherein one possesses a direct identity with one acts, Sartre is reinforcing the radical importance of the Other. In order to underscore this he highlights how this non-thetic consciousness is the character of the situation: "This ensemble in the world with its double and inverted determinations (there is a spectacle to be seen behind the door only because I am jealous, but my jealousy is nothing except the simple objective fact that *there is* a sight *to be seen* behind the door)—this we shall call *situation*." This situation reflects to me at once both my facticity and my freedom; on the occasion of a certain objective structure of the world which surrounds me, it refers to my freedom in the form of tasks to be done"[22]

.

One issue that arises here is the one that Kathleen Wilder develops as the basis of her critique of Sartre's philosophy, wondering how it that non-thetic consciousness can serve as the basis of anything. However, this position represents an abstraction of Sartre's ontology in that non-thetic consciousness represents a specific type of recognition of the other, as Sartre described in his depiction of "the Look." Furthermore, as we discussed in the earlier analysis of *Mit-sein*, there is a layering effect of one's intentional moments that is part and parcel of a relational ontology not only in terms of transcendental phenomenology, but that is so by virtue of the immanence of being for-itself and being in-itself. If that were not the case, then bad faith would not be described by Sartre as an attempt to exploit this duality of consciousness as immanence and transcendence. Additionally, for Sartre, the 'subject' does not exist prior to consciousness and this has consequences at the level of the everyday, where non-thetic consciousness merely refers to the fact that one always exists in a situation. In sum, non-thetic consciousness represents the status of one as always already in a *situation*.

Sartre's analysis of what happens when the 'Other' sees one is depicted by him as a fundamental reversal in the existential field: "Thus originally the bond between my unreflective consciousness and my *Ego*, which is being looked at, is a bond, not of knowing, but of being. Beyond any knowledge which I can have, I am this self which another knows. And this self which I am—this I am in a world which the 'Other' has made alien to me, for the 'Others' look embraces my being and correlatively the walls, the door, the keyhole. All these instrumental-things, in the midst of which I am, now turn toward the 'Other' a face which on principle escapes me. Thus I am my *Ego* for the 'Other' in the midst of a world which (now) flows toward the Other."[23] Sartre sums up the political importance of this aspect of being-for-Others this way: "Everything takes place as if I had a dimension of being from which I was separated by a radical nothingness: and this nothingness is the 'Others' freedom. The 'Other' has to make my being-for-him *be* in so far as he has to be his being. Thus, each of my free conducts engages me in a new environment where the very stuff of my being is the unpredictable freedom of another."[24] So, this is a different approach to the question of 'obligation' and 'responsibility' than the one offered in the de-ontological account. There, it will be recalled, the emphasis is upon acting according to the role prescribed by citizenship, for example, or acceptance of an implicit social contract. For Sartre, however, there is a prior 'obligation' and 'responsibility' and it involves recognition in an immediate, direct and ontological way. In other words, the ethics of recognition is prior to its derived formulations.

Let us now return to considering how Sartre presents this issue in his play, *The Flies*. So, we have a plague. Bad faith is the condition under which the citizens live, and there is an attendant ideology to go along with it, so as to set in place and reinforce the idea that it was the act of Clytemnestra and Aigisthos, in actuality the effect, that caused the plague and not their own agency.

NOTES

1. Sartre, op. cit., 1966: 318.

2. Ibid.: 320.

3. Ibid.: 321.

4. The author would like to cite Jay Bernstein for very helpful expository suggestions regarding this aspect of Sartre's ontology

5. The context for Heidegger's analysis, of course, is the discussion of "care," and its role in the "call of conscience." In the first instance, what Heidegger refers to as authentic being-towards-death comes about through the agency of moods such as dread and anxiety. These basic and revealing moods are themselves a part of Dasein's pre-understanding of Being, and as such they are, to a certain extent, pre-cognitive as well. Dasein's faculty for discerning the pre-understanding of his ownmost potentiality for not-being is the category of 'care' itself. 'Care,' in fact, is pre-ontological and reflects the fact, and is in turn reflected by, Dasein's status as 'thrown-being.' Dasein is, according to Heidegger, born with the pre-understanding of Being as part and parcel of its already (given) horizon, and Dasein ultimately cannot do otherwise than make present its own presentness. In addition, one becomes aware of one's condition through the 'uncanniness' of being-in-the-world. The question of disclosure then, is not only a matter of correctly deciphering the history of Being, or its present moment as the hermeneutical interpretation suggests, but is, instead, in *Being and Time*, tantamount to being established on the basis of something prior to language. For, "uncanniness" represents the key moments in which authentic *angst* and not fear (being specific) brings Dasein face to face with its condition of being or nothing. One can 'escape' from this freedom, as Fromm and Becker note, and through recourse to specific strategies within average-everydayness. Or, one can project one's self in the manner described by Heidegger, that is, as authentic projection. But the question of how this takes place *sans* human agency is a serious flaw

6. On this score, the correspondence between Heidegger and Sartre is quite telling. On this score, one can read Sartre's play *No Exit* as precisely a satire of the Heideggerian depiction of death. It is hard to imagine a more banal, less authentic set of characters than the ones Sartre introduces in *No Exit*.

7. Heidegger does not use the term *alienation*. Its presence here is not meant to suggest that Heidegger was interested in the "subject," but rather that the use of Being and Time for political theory contains a flaw: an inability to address what is a central problem of political thought: political alienation itself.

8. Sartre, op. cit., 1966: 468-469

9. Ibid.: 152.

10. In the case of Husserl, this is discussed at the outset of Section sixty-three in Ideas II, where Husserl draws attention to the fact that a subject is a person that be-

longs to many groupings such being a citizen within a state and can thereby relate to others on the basis of recognition or compassion as one would toward others. Indeed, it could also be said that the 'natural' attitude is in need of bracketing as an ethical caveat. For, implicit in the 'natural' attitude is the tendency to treat individuals possibly as specimens, or other 'objects'.

11. Sartre, op. cit., 1966: 152.

12. Ibid.: 152-53.

13. One illustration of the reifying of such categories is the neo-liberal lexicon of a marketplace of ideas as though structures were reducible merely to the "exchange" of ideas. This tendency in contemporary ideology extends to the emphasis placed on values and ethical perspectives separated from their political context. On this score, Ruth Sample's work, *Exploitation: What it is and Why It's Wrong* is a good example of this tendency. Despite its positive message, it, like so many in the genre, assumes that exploitation is merely a matter of individual will as opposed to also being an immanent structure of political economy.

14. Hazel Barnes, "Sartre and the Emotions," In *Philosophy, Politics and Ethics*, ed. William McBride (New York: Garland 1968): xviii-xix.

15. This is an issue that surfaces in the debate between Sartre and Merleau-Ponty. The issue concerns the relationship and scope of politics. For Sartre, there simply is no escape from the need to engage in politics. It is, in short, an inescapable feature of Reality. Merleau- Ponty, on the other hand, while certainly establishing himself as a political actor, nevertheless believed in a realm of existence—akin to Arendt's private sphere—wherein the Arts and the Humanities, including philosophy, take root and develop outside of the realm of 'the political.' This issue is writ large in the formal break between Merleu-Ponty and Sartre, captured in "Philosophy and Political Engagement: Letters from the Quarrel Between Sartre and Merleu-Ponty," in *The Debate Between Sartre and Merleu-Ponty*, Jon Stewart ed., (Evanston: Northwestern University Press, 1998).A separate, but related issue here is the consideration of the position that theorizing, including philosophy, is a form of action.

16. Heidegger's interpretation of the "Anaximander Fragment," involves in its English translation the idea of 'wreck' as opposed to 'letting-be,' an expression that he returns to repeatedly and which itself has overtones to certain ideas in Eastern philosophy. Nietzsche, whose translation Heidegger discusses in his analysis of the "Anaximander Fragment," seems closer to the overall spirit of presocratic politics.

17. Some obvious exceptions, of course, are Rousseau, Hegel and Marx.

18. Sartre, op. cit., 1966: 56.

19. Ibid.: 315.

20. Ibid.: 317.

21. Ibid.: 318.

22. Ibid.: 320.

23. Ibid.: 321.

Chapter Six

Sartre's Account of Social Evil in *The Flies*

THE INTENTIONALITY OF FREEDOM
IN SARTRE'S EARLY LITERARY WORKS

Sartre's theory of evil is sometimes glossed as though it were a mere literary device. For example, his account of hell in his play No Exit is one of the most famous. Yet, the phrase "Hell is the Other," has become something of a mantra that is repeated at the mention of Sartre often with the result that what he actually has to say about evil is dismissed. He was far too good of a writer perhaps and so for the most part his legacy in this area has been reduced to a pithy sound-byte. However, it is an important aspect of the overall attempt to rethink what Sartre's philosophy has to say, and this especially so since it concerns nothing less than the relationship between individual existence and the social order. For Sartre this relationship can become a social pathology as that he explains how this takes place in both his formal works as well as in his literary ones like his play *The Flies*. However, it is essential to recall that Sartre's account of his social pathology is located not in the positivist discourse of behavior and rights but in the context of consciousness as a being-in-the-world. It is difficult to fully appreciate the full power or the consequences of what Sartre has to say on this topic without a full understanding of the idea of being-with-others as a way of being-in-the-world. For that reason it is necessary to recall some other texts that examine this issue and here one key text is that of Heidegger's analysis of the they-self (*das Mann*) of average-everydayness. His structure of human existence is explained by Heidegger as merely one of the ways that *Dasein* is in the world. So it is for Heidegger one way among many others to be sure, but nevertheless with its own unusual stamp. In brief, here is what he has to say about it: Heidegger locates the problem in his discussion of being-with and in particular the relationship between being-with-one-another and what he terms the "they-self." The term "they-self" denotes the public persona of the individual. Heidegger maintains that the ontological mode of the "they-self" is structural in that even when *Dasein* is not in public, the interpretations, ideas, values and importantly, one's behaviors, are all traceable to the structure of the "they-self" of average-everydayness. Yet, because Dasein is a being that is concerned (with its own being), it is "absorbed in the world of its concern" (Ibid). Proceeding, Dasein finds itself in the following circumstance: At the same time (as it is concerned with its world), in its Being-with towards 'Others', Dasein finds that not only is it that Dasein is, as Kockelmans noted above, disguised with respect to Being, but it is also disguised with regard to itself as well. We may say that this state of affairs represents *Dasein's* alienation. However, one might ask, given the corporate identity of the they-self of average everydayness how can the individual ever come to realize that they are alienated since the they-self is a structure of existence that "dominates" the individual. This condition extends even to one's behaviors. For, as Heidegger notes when speaking of the agency that is involved in the they-self, when the question comes up as to who's ideas they are that one is acting on, it invariably turns out that they are the anonymous ones of the they-self and agency as such all but disappears.

In addition, it should also be noted that the 'they-self' has an uncanny character that distinguishes it from anomie. For Heidegger says further that it is nothing less than a takeover of one's individual existence. On this score, one takes pleasure and enjoy one's self as *they* take pleasure, one reads, sees, and judges literature and art as *they* see and judge" (Ibid). It seems that on this account that Dasein's capacity as a being that can interpret, let alone critique, is severely undermined.[1] This condition is thoroughly existential in that the they-self covers over everything that is basic about the human condition, things that truly should matter to people are trivialized under the rubric of phraseology.

In terms of the tradition and legacy of this account the obvious connection to the powerful novel and film *Lord of the Flies* captures the problem of amoral human agency in the hypothetical situation of a closed society and how the Other is generated through bad faith in a collective self-negation of each individual's personhood. Earlier still, one could cite the behaviors and words of Job's interlocutors in the *Book of Job*. Also in this tradition is of course other works such as Dostoyevsky's "Grand Inquisitor" from the *Brothers Karamazov*.

Now that this analysis has introduced the historical context for Sartre's account of social evil the focus will move towards providing an exposition and an analysis of some of Sartre's theory of alienation in two of his early literary works. Our purpose in doing so is to highlight the implications of Sartre's doctrine of Intentionality, including its Realism and concept of freedom, for political thought. As we saw earlier, in several key passages in Sartre's novel *Nausea*, he provides an existential account of what is a mainstay of his political thought: The idea that there is an ideology of the everyday and that the experience of it brings with it the challenge of bad faith. In his play, *The Flies*, this idea is expanded upon and we read that the opposition to this form of ideology puts one at odds with established authority, including political authority.

In addition to *Nausea,* however, Sartre provides an even more explicit account of this political dilemma in his play, *The Flies*. In it, the issue of the challenge of existential freedom is posed of course, but it is presented as an opposition to the established authorities or god and the state, personified as Zeus and Aegistheus. Before proceeding to our exposition of these points, a few additional remarks may be useful.

One effect of Sartre's depiction of bad faith is that it politicizes the phenomenological view of reality—the idea of the given. This is because, in the first instance, the phenomenology of the experienced world is one that is in every instance already given, of course, but it also refers, in the case of Sartre, to the fact that there is something politically challenging to the established political order by an individual who is aware and living in their existential freedom. Again, here we are not referring to the engaged political actor that Sartre champions in his later political writings, but rather to the individual who fits the pattern Sartre describes in Orestes. On this score, however, such individuals, by virtue of their existential comportment, almost invariably also come into conflict with the political order and established authority generally. Overall, they come to be viewed as dissidents.

THE IDEOLOGY OF THE EVERYDAY WORLD

For Sartre, overcoming established politics as it is presented in everyday life involves depicting ideology as far more than that of merely being a phenomenon that evinces social or political ideas and values. Ideology for Sartre begins when a depiction of reality entirely avoids the problem of this primary problem of existence *per se*. Perhaps the most universal political expression of this position is the tendency, especially within political ideology, to posit political causes as effect and political effects as cause. This tendency all but defines ideology as Sartre uses it. In his later works, of course, Sartre comes much closer to the classical definition of ideology. However, here, where we are considering bad faith and its influence on ideology and politics, bad faith may be construed as a kind of individual ideology (as opposed to an ideology of the individual), in which by positing itself as an essence, it gives rise to behaviors. For Sartre, in doing so, one reverses the actual relationship that is at work in one's being-in-the-world: The idea that one is both immanence and transcendence relative to the world. It is lastly, for this reason that most instances of bad faith, to the extent that they involve activity of some kind, are also instances wherein what is in fact an effect, is depicted as a cause. As has often enough been noted, for Sartre, the everyday depiction of reality is already abstracted one step from the phenomenon of existence: the Intentionality of consciousness. Sartre assessment of the "pseudo-concrete" is that the latter are nothing less than the abstract and reified forms of social relationships. The human need for love and affection either in the family or outside of it is separate and apart from the various ideologies that in some cases distort those relationships. However, once again it is the intentionality of human freedom that is the actual basis of all of these ideologies and constructs and it is this that constitutes the starting point for human dignity and not the various subjectivities and ideologies that are celebrated instead of human freedom.

One example that was often used by Sartre to convey this was the difference between living and acting the role that one's situation places one in. The passage, at the end of his novel *Nausea* where he is bidding goodbye to the members of the grand bourgeois that line the museum underscores the dissonance between the living individual and the stance, or posture they adopt as part of the performance of their role. Sartre is careful to distinguish the relationships that comprise the family from the ideology of the family. For Sartre the ideology of the family is evinced nowhere more persistently, nor falsely than in the way the upper class presents itself to the working class, as the famous final scene from *Nausea* evinces.

For Sartre, one of the most effective ways to get to the essence of 'reification' was to present the issue in a literary context. Placing the 'pseudo-concrete' side by side with his own phenomenological ontology makes his critique more complete. One may, for example, read *Nausea* as a depiction of alienation in mass society. In order to highlight this point, and to "totalize" it. Sartre presents the following portrait of the alienated individual, on the one hand, and the life of custom, tradition, conformity, the 'pseudo-concrete,' and everyday ideology including the distinction between family and ideology.

> "I had forgotten that this morning was Sunday. I went out and walked along the streets as usual. . . . Then, suddenly, when opening the gate of the public park I got the impression that something was signaling to me. The park was bare and deserted. But . . . how can I explain?

It didn't have its usual look, it smiled at me. I leaned against the railing for a moment then suddenly realized it was Sunday. It was there – on the trees, on the grass, like a faint smile . . .

Its Sunday: behind the docks, along the seacoast, near the freight station, all around the city there are empty warehouses and motionless machines in the darkness. In all the houses men are shaving behind their windows, sometimes they stare at the looking glass, sometimes at the sky to see if it's going to be a fine day. . . In all the suburbs, between the interminable walls of factories, long black processions have started walking; they are slowing advancing towards the center of the town.

A clock strikes half-past ten and I start on my way: Sundays, at this hour, you can see a fine show in Bouville, but you must not come too late after High Mass.

You must not be in a hurry in the Rue Tournebride: the families walk slowly. Sometimes you move up a step because a family has turned into Foulon's or Piegeois'. But, at other times, you must stop and mark time because two families, one going up the street and the other coming down have met and have solidly clasped hands. I go forward slowly. I stand a whole head above both columns and I see hats, a sea of hats. . . .

The bell of the Cine-Eldorado resounded in the clear air. This is familiar Sunday noise, this ringing in broad daylight. More then a hundred people were lining up along the green wall. They were greedily awaiting the hour of soft shadows, of relaxation, abandon, the hour when the screen, glowing like a white stone under water, would speak and dream for them . . . Soon, as every other Sunday, they would be disappointed . . . Soon, as on every other Sunday, small mute rages would grow in the darkened hall."[2]

In the passage we can discern the prior sense of politics that is evinced in Sartre's early account of alienation. For, the issue of bad faith is writ large even in everyday or mundane activities generally considered to be *apolitical*.[3] Thus, the mental state of Roquinten, the main character in *Nausea* does not represent an attempt to place the alienated individual and his psyche in the context of existing social norms, and then to abstractly assess those norms. Instead, Sartre depicts both his character's alienation and that of the society that surrounds him, as evincing a prior instance of alienation. Of course, one can press an objection here and maintain that contrary to this view, it seems that this simply a representation of an alienated individual and it may not be taken as evidence of an alienated society.

Furthermore, along these lines, one could argue that in order for the passage to reflect alienation and not the problems of an individual's abnormal psychology over and against established social norms, one would first need to establish the relationship between alienation and the original organization of society, as Rousseau did in *The Social Contract*, for example. One would have to work backwards, in other words, and start with some type of specific pathology or other expression of alienation. However, in response, one could point out that Sartre has already done this through his depiction of bad faith. In fact, the latter comprises the whole point Sartre is making about the plague that afflicts the citizens of Argos. The everyday experience of ideology is added onto the Intentionality of consciousness. So, there are two elements in Sartre's depiction of political reality. They are the ideology of the everyday and bad faith. With regard to the former, we saw that in the passage from *Nausea* cited above that Sartre takes note of the implicit, albeit sublimated violence that attends the onset of the weekly work cycle. Throughout the work there are scores of satirical references to the capitalist class of Bouville. One example of this is that the chief vice that Roquinten accuses the city of is not its exploitation, or even the extent to which class relations have deformed its residents, but rather the extent to which most citizens are unaware of precisely how absurd their position actually is. In terms of alienation, the condition of *nausea*, outlined in Sartre's novel, represents the following irony: That it is not the individual who experiences the *nausea* that is alienated. Rather, it is the 'Others' who are unaware of alienation.

For Sartre, solving the problem of alienation begins with an analysis of bad faith. Earlier, we saw that bad faith was described as a form of dis-recognition, or adopting a negative stance towards one's self. One passage that is particularly relevant to the relationship between the ideology of the everyday and bad faith is the scene in *Nausea* where Roquentin experiences a moment of epiphany. In it he sees the connection between his bad faith the reification of his biographical project. When the character Roquentin goes to the museum to research his subject his emotions alert him to a certain uncanny feeling. The difficulty, it turns out, is that the pedestal, symbolic of the position of the bourgeois, and, by extension the past, is not only too grand for the individual placed upon it, but appears disjointed owing to the actual history of Bouville, a history he knows both from his research and from his having lived there. It is this insight, or if one prefers, intuition, that acts as the catalyst for the unraveling of Roquentin's tightly woven assembly of received ideas. Sartre uses the image of the pedestal from *Nausea* to provide a literary account of history and reification, in which the pedestal itself may be viewed as a symbol of power exercised through political culture. Throughout the work the present is continually imposing itself on Roquintin, even as he attempts to salve his psyche by immersion in the study of the past. However, the past of local Bouville history and also his own biographical reflections are of little use to him owing to his bad faith. In other words, there is a 'bad-faith' version of the attempt to *totalize* one's situation and it is marked by a philosophical attempt to totalize the past by imposing the present on it. When this is the case, invariably the result is that one mistakes cause for effect. Sartre works out the mechanism of this from a political vantage point in his later writings. However, the idea is present even in his early works. Again, these are instances of bad-faith because for Sartre, the present includes the texture of existence, and Sartre reminds his reader that it can never be limited in the way Rouquentin intends to do through the pursuit of a kind of pseudo history. Roquinten's inspection of his biographical project, since it involves a local celebrity, has echoes in the contemporary fixation on celebrity and their lifestyles and so on. Sartre uses the specter of a pedestal to convey the simple idea, an absurd one in his writings, of sacrificing one's authentic abilities and interests in order to do homage to celebrities be they those of the Nineteenth-Century or more modern ones. The rejection of celebrity is a core aspect of Sartre's indictment of the hidden faces of ideology, of which his refusal of the Nobel Prize is an instantiation.

Sartre's argument in his version of Aeschylus' trilogy, *The Orestia*, is that human alienation and agency represent the initial or fundamental experience of being human. Or, to put the matter differently, He is arguing that the fundamental experience of human existence is political. Here, we want to underscore this point, return specifically to *Nausea* and *The Flies* because the exposition of these works acts as a counterweight to the view that alienation and politics were issues of preoccupation for Sartre only after his rethinking of socialism, something one finds primarily in his mature works.

In its original form, *The Orestia* by Aeschylus depicts the familiar Greek concern with violence begetting violence, interrupted eventually only by the intervention and agency of the gods. Also, in Aeschylus' version, a new paradigm of justice needed to be introduced, the tribunal, in order for the violence of the family, and by extension the community, to come to an end. Sartre's interpretation is considerably different. His interpretation underscores not only his early political philosophy, but also the contours of the differences in approach between his assessment of the Presocratics and, most especially, that of Heidegger. For Sartre, the Intentionality of consciousness is closely related to the guilt of the citizens of Argos. For, even as each citizen attempts to hide bad faith behind a veil of ignorance, the very fact of consciousness (as de-centered and in the world), necessitates that this defense, the traditional one, is utterly without merit. At the outset of his play, Sartre uses the example of an old woman whose pretense of ignorance regarding the murder of King Agamemnon hints at the role of ideology, as a mistaking of cause for effect, in continuing the plague that has now beset the community. For, not only was it the case (as is brought out during the interrogation of the old woman by Zeus), that the old woman remembered the actual history of the crime committed by Clytemnestra and her lover, Aegistheus, and is thus guilty of lying about her knowledge, but she is also guilty by virtue of her continued reinforcement of the ideology of the royal myth—by her participating in the annual ritual that legitimizes the existing royalty. Finally, she is guilty for acquiescing to the official 'story' of the event and for reinforcing it among others including the young. We can see this in Sartre's rendering of an encounter with Zeus:

Zeus: Now, old lady, let's hear your tale of woe. I see you're in black from head to foot. In mourning for a whole regiment of sons, is that it? Tell us—and I'll release you—perhaps. For whom are you in mourning?

Old Woman: Sir, I am not in mourning. Everyone wears black at Argos.

Zeus: Everyone wears black? Ah, I see. You're in mourning for your murdered King.

Old Woman: Whisht! For God's sake, don't talk of that.

Zeus: Yes, you're quite old enough to have heard those huge cries that echoed and re-echoed for a whole morning in the city streets. What did you do about it? (Sartre, 1977, pp. 71-72)

For Sartre, the initial crime here is related to Mit-sein: This is underscored throughout the play, but perhaps nowhere more directly than in the following passage:

Zeus: All crimes do not displease me equally. And now, Aegistheus, I shall speak to you frankly, as one king to another. The first crime was mine; I committed it when I made man mortal. Once I had done that, what was left for you, poor human murders to do? To kill your victims? But they already had the seed of death in them; all you had to do was to hasten its fruition by a year or two. . . But your crime served my ends.

Aegistheus: What ends? For fifteen years I have been atoning for it—and you say it served your ends!

Zeus: Exactly. It's because you are atoning for it that it served my ends. I like crimes that pay. I like yours because it was a clumsy, boorish murder, a crime that did not know itself, a crime in the antique mode, more like a cataclysm than an act of man. Not for a moment did you defy me. You struck in a frenzy of fear and rage. And then, when your frenzy had died down, you looked back on the deed with loathing and disowned it. Yet what profit I have made on it! For one dead man, twenty thousand living men wallow in penitence. Yes, it was a good bargain I struck that day. (Sartre, 1977: 132)

As a reified entity, the gods are threatened by the plague, but in reverse. For both the king and the deity are equiprimordially threatened by man's agency.

Zeus: You may hate me, but we are akin: I made you in my image. A king is a god on earth, glorious and terrifying as a god.

Aegistheus: You terrifying?

Zeus: Look at me (a long silence). I told you you were made in my image. Each keeps order; you in Argos, I in heaven and on earth—and you and I harbor the same dark secret in our hearts.

Aegistheus: I have no secret.

Zeus: You have. The same as mine. The bane of gods and kings. The bitterness of knowing men are free. Yes Aegistheus, they are free. But your subjects do not know it, and you do."[4]

Like Rouquinten in Sartre's novel, *Nausea*, Sartre's Orestes is acutely aware of this initial state of alienation because he is aware of the actual history that gave rise to the plague. Here we can reflect on the fact that one of the main problems with positivist approaches to political theory is their insistence on what is actionable in the present. In other words, positivism bypasses the historical roots of the plague and yet these are precisely the roots that Orestes is acutely conscious of. Sartre emphasizes this aspect of history as truly political history when he introduces a discourse by Orestes in which he tries to raise the historical memories at the heart of the plague.

Orestes: . . . But, mind you, if there were something I could do, something to give me the freedom of the city; if, even by a crime, I could acquire their memories, their hopes and fears, and fill with these the void within me, yes, even if I had to kill my own mother—

Furthermore, for Sartre, we see that the Greek idea of a primordial *strife* is described by him as alienation of consciousness as Intentional. It is interesting to note that both Zeus and Aegistheus have a passion for order, Sartre tells us:

Aegistheus: Alas! But who has doomed us?

Zeus: No one but ourselves. For we have the same passion. You Aegistheus, have, like me, a passion for order.

Aegistheus: For order? That is so. It was for the sake of order that I wooed Clytemnestra, for order that I killed my King; I wished that order should prevail, and that it should prevail through me. I have lived without love, without hope, even without lust. But I have kept order. Yes, I have kept good order in my kingdom. That has been my ruling passion; a godlike passion, but how terrible.[5]

Sartre's Orestes is dangerous to this order, but not merely because his freedom and lack of political socialization make him a subversive to Argos, a committed political actor, but also because his existential freedom is a threat to the 'given' as already political. The legitimacy of the gods may be taken as the legitimacy of the established ideology even while that ideology is hidden as simply "the ways things are" or even, as noted earlier, or according to some interpretations, in the "state of nature."

This initial plague, of course, of which both king and god are fearful, is the original intent through which the recognition of the individual as the agent of his own destiny is established. To a certain extent then, Sartre answers Heidegger's interpretation of the Presocratics by arguing that the mystery that must consume man is not the mystery of Being's address to Dasein, but rather it is the case that the mystery consists in the intentionality of consciousness and the fact that it is alienated from itself as a condition for its existence.

NOTES

1. The tradition has tended to emphasize the influence of Kierkegaard in this section of Heidegger's analysis of alienation. On this score, it is worth noting that for Kierkegaard the problem of the liberation of human existence from a primary alienation as the human condition, takes place through the agency of God. This is not a part of Heidegger's argument however

2. Sartre, 1964: 59-72).

3. It is important to note that the point of this particular passage is not the isolated individual but instead, as noted, what Hegel refers to as the individual as universal, one who may possess abnormal psychology (as Roquinten does), but who nevertheless, as an individual who grasps the truth about, in this instance, mass society, (a 'totalized' perspective), and hence is in possession of the most 'true' perspective. In Hegelian parlance, such an individual *grasps* the immediate reality conceptually, and consequently, has the most accurate view of it.

4. Sartre, op. cit., 1946: 133-134.

5. Ibid.: 82-135.

Chapter Seven

Political History in
The Critique of Dialectical Reason

In this final section of our analysis we will consider the case that Sartre makes in his late work, *The Critique of Dialectical Reason* for scarcity as driving force in history and the source of human praxis. It is an important argument because what Sartre is arguing is that the single most important source of human negativities is the reality of scarcity and its existence as a condition that is overcome through praxis. Obviously this view stands directly opposed to the view put forth by ideologies that place the emphasis on inherent human traits or still worse on lack of character. It is surprising that in the new millennium there are still many voices, many of them held in high esteem within the academy, who openly claims that one of the reasons why democracy cannot be universally promoted, leaving aside for the moment whether it actually has been, is that some societies lack the temperament and the character for democracy. Sartre is the preeminent spokesperson for the opposing view and in his works on anti-colonialism and neo-colonialism he takes up these claims and undermines them in due course. However, his more sustained critique of the foundations of the ideology of history is found in his late philosophical work, *The Critique of Dialectical Reason*. In it he argues that far from it being the case that social negativities as the result of the actualization of an inherent predisposition and various genetic profile of one form or another, they actually grow out of the condition of scarcity. His concept of scarcity is thoroughly historical however and in order to fully appreciate it we need to place his theory of history in its appropriate critical context.

The result of ahistorical ideology is a kind of collective amnesia the results of which are the continuation, in ideological form, of the original state that brought it about. So Sartre is insisting that we get it right with regard to history before we begin to offer causal explanations for why the political world is the way it is. Sartre famously rejects the idea of human nature and we can begin to appreciate the strong role that he assigns to history if we consider his explication of it in his study of anti-Semitism wherein Sartre notes the importance of beginning with the idea, not of human nature, but of the historical situation. He asks, not what a Jew is, but: "What have you made of the Jews." In doing so, Sartre is drawing attention to the actual history of anti-Semitism. This involves an insistence of politics in place of the ideology of religion. At the same time, he is also underscoring the psycho-social role played by an historical Other: "Primarily, as we have seen, anti-Semitism is the expression of a primitive society that, through secret and diffused, remains latent in the legal collectivity. We must not suppose, therefore, that generous outpouring of emotion, a few pretty words, and a stroke of the pen will suffice to suppress it. That would be like imagining you could abolish war by denouncing its effects in a book."[1] In a similar way Sartre brings this point home in his introduction to Franz Fanon's work, The Wretched of the Earth when he exposes the objective conditions that inform the colonial practice of co-opting and re-socializing colonialized peoples.

It is difficult to make sense of colonialism or anti-Semitism without an understanding of the practices that inform the relationship between politics and ideology. For Sartre as we saw in his play *The Flies*. There is a ruse by which actual politics and real political circumstances, that is historical politics, is replaced by the creation of ideology. For Sartre, this pattern recurs under various auspices. It is worth pursuing whether or not the selfsame replacement of actual politics; that is to say, engagement and recognition over actual differences, is substituted for an ideology that serves as a template for bad faith.

For Sartre, one of the main characteristics of this ruse is that scarcity is sublimated into ideology by way of a kind of sublimation of the earlier reality, including the political one. The earlier bad faith is then a reflection of the earlier politics of scarcity but now as an ideology that may contain racist overtones or code words and other references to essentialist identities. For Sartre, the decisive element that is an often overlooked feature of his depiction of the "politics of the Other" is the relationship between bad faith and scarcity. To be more specific, bad faith engenders an inaccurate rendering of the nature of the Other because the other is experienced through the mediation of scarcity. Of course, critics of Sartre often point out that not all experiences of the other are mediated by the realities of scarcity and, in his earlier formulations, the category of *Mit-sein*. Relationships of love and affection have little or nothing to do with such assessments is thereby, outside of the realm of ideology. However, it is rare indeed that the socialization process does not enter into decisions regarding whom to choose as one's life partner. These decisions may in fact be authentic but that does not discount the tremendous pull that scarcity exerts on human relationships. Ideology is a secondary construct developed on the basis of bad faith and it, in its turn, is a reflection of scarcity. Instead of turning a negative stance towards myself or the Other, the hallmarks of bad faith, in ideology I turn this towards the Others in general. As Sartre puts it in his study of colonialism, it is those Algerians, it is they who are the inferior ones, whereas we Westerners, we are the superior ones, and we are so, one might add by essence. Here again, Sartre's approach is not merely to concentrate on the discourses and activities of colonialism but rather the elemental forms through which it is experienced and then inscribed in the landscape of, in the case, Algeria's politics. As he notes, "But on the other hand, and conversely, since the elementary structures of the simplest forms are inscribed in inorganic matter, they refer to various activities (both past and present) which either indefinitely reproduce or have helped to produce these human *seals* as inert thoughts: and these activities are necessarily antagonistic. The racism which occurs to an Algerian colonialist was imposed and produced by the conquest of Algeria, and is constantly recreated and reactualized by everyday practice through serial alterity."[2] One way of describing or looking at ideology then is through the history that continues to present itself as a feature of the practico-inert and not merely as a system of ideas that can easily be dislodged presumably by truthful ones.

Sartre's implicit depiction of ideology contains the following nuance: He is not arguing that ideology is a *pseudo* category *per se*. Instead, his argument is merely that it is one step removed from being the most basic. Thus for example, citizens may be depicted as apathetic and yet the deeper political question is why the apathy exists. What is at issue here is the relationship, once again, between epistemology and politics, for the simultaneous positing of ideologies positivist explanations of political conditions has the effect of bracketing the level of *praxis* as an historical category.

Sartre's account of social and political reality is one wherein causality is established in more radical way than in most other accounts. Here the word radical is meant to suggest a deeper level of analysis. Sartre is arguing that the condition of scarcity sets in motion a possible response that will cause one to overcome what is the normal state of affairs—concern with one's own individual consciousness—and enact a series of projects with others. Sartre calls this activity praxis and it is to be distinguished from alterity in which one follows the dominant ideology and is passive with regard to the structures that create and reinforce the condition of scarcity. In other words, Sartre is not contesting the idea of the individual and positing a notion of the community as prior to the individual. Instead, his approach involves showing that the initial state of affairs wherein the individual is focused on their own consciousness is not a state that it immutable. There is in fact quite a bit to recommend this point, for in fact in the politics of social movements it is often the case that after the goals of a social movement are accomplished the members of the movement return to the default of individual consciousness. In other words, something extraordinary has to happen in order for individuals to wrenched out of their everyday world and place on the path to, what Sartre calls the *group-in-fusion*.

The circumstances must be all the more extraordinary in a culture that is a heavily imbued with the ideology of the individual subject as America is. And for Sartre there is nothing axiomatic about the transformation of consciousness from individual consciousness to the *group-in-fusion* since social action remains an existential category. Thus, it is just as likely that individuals will engage in quietism as it is that they will initiate social action. True, as the social movement theorists underscore, the existence of a grievance is necessary, but it is not sufficient because the kind of acquiesce he describes as *alterity* remains a possible, or really the more probable choice. We can see the point that Sartre is making here if we contrast it with a mainstay of political theory, the prisoner's dilemma. In the account of the prisoner's dilemma it is individual self-interest and self-interest as a calculative thought process that is decisive. Thus in a hypothetical situation, that of an individual who is trying to decide whether to join with others in a union, the individual will make his or her decision on the basis of a certain calculus of self-interest. For Sartre such actions involve the entire person, their passions and sense or lack thereof, of recognition and these decisions will be mediated by history itself. History will impose itself on the situation not only by such things as the history of the grievance, labor unions, earlier victories by Capital in undermining or elimination unions, but also by the physical landscape of politics, by what Sartre refers to as the *practico-inert*. An example of the *practico-inert* in our example would be something like the courts. Here we are referring not merely to the judges and lawyers, some of whom may or may not be sympathetic, but to the actual brick and mortar – the visual sight of the courts and the associated nomenclature—the legal briefs, and injunctions, the subpoenas and the like. All of this too has a history and it imposes itself on the situation confronted by the individual worker. For example, in a recent New York City transit workers strike the legal maneuverings of the City of New York and the daily publication of the court's proceedings exerted a political influence on the agency of the workers and the union itself. The background was lit, so to speak, by the decades-old Taylor Laws, laws that were put into effect to suppress labor's only real tool—the strike. So the entire complex of legal proceedings, including the documents, the citations, the courts and the participants reflected the practico-inert and its influence on present day politics. It is literally the manifestation of the politics of history.

Another example of the practio-inert, also from the history of labor politics, is the presence of those huge and intimidating buildings that are found in most of the major cities of the Northeastern United States. These armories, Jereamy Brecher tells us in his book, Strike, were built to house federal troops stationed for the purpose of suppressing strikes during the late Nineteenth Century, a period of extraordinary labor activism in the Unites States. Sartre wants us to think about these structures both the physical ones and the invisible ones as reflections of earlier struggles against the human condition of unfreedom and scarcity. These social movement struggles may be in abeyance or may have even resulted in victory, the continued presence of this residue of politics continues to exert an influence and to make its presence felt.

Progressive Praxis also has a history of course and it emerges when historical grievances reappear. For example, social movement scholars often note that in American politics the tendency is for successful social movements to form themselves into interest groups, achieve a seat at the table, and influence public policy through interest groups organizing and lobbying. A trade off is made in which the leaderships gives up direct action and mass mobilization in the streets and takes on the accoutrements of an interest group. However, if the interest group is unsuccessful or has in some way been undermined, the possibility exists that a reversion to the politics of social movement activism can reappear and the positive praxis will confront the historical forces it was once successful against.

For Sartre one's situation is infused with history but by this he is not only referring to events, ideas and patterns of socialization but to the world that one is situated in *per se*. So as we saw above in our discussion of the armories in the major cities of the Northeast this category includes the so-called objective order as well. One experiences existence as a social context, however, it is a social context that is defined in the first instance as alienating. The context of political economy provides the historical contours of *Mit-sein* but only on the foundation of Sartean freedom, nor its expression in human agency: "Thus alienation can modify the *results* of an action but not its profound reality. We refuse to confuse the alienated man with a thing or alienation with the physical laws governing external conditions. We affirm the specificity of the human act, which cuts across the social milieu while still holding on to its determinations, and which transforms the world on the basis of given conditions. For us man is characterized above all by his going beyond a situation, and by what he succeeds in making of what he has been made—even if he never recognizes himself in his objectification. This going beyond we find at the very root of the human—in *need*." The refusal of which Sartre speaks is the refusal to accept the behavioral model or the deterministic one which might tend to place a mediation before the structure of intentional experience, or what is the same, the priority of being-in-the-world *per se*. Sartre is also underscoring the three-fold relationship among *Mit-sein*, history and freedom, in his analysis of the different social relationships one sees various cultures. The appearance of any particular social institution is at once a relationship to history, to 'Others' and to one's own freedom as evinced in a project: "For this scarcity is not a simple lack; in its most naked form it expresses a situation in society and contains already an effort to go beyond it. The most rudimentary behavior must be determined both in relation to the real and present factors which condition it and the relation to a certain object, still to come, which it is trying to bring into being. This is what we call *the project*."[3] Here it is worth recalling that from an existential point of view it is the project as well as the attention that it implies, that provides the unity that we eventually come to recognize as the subject. The knowledge of the relationship among *Mit-sein*, history and freedom is itself susceptible to alienation. For, in terms of the specificity of the human experience of alienation, Sartre cites the classical formulation provided by Marx: "Creative work is alienated; man does not recognize himself in his own product, and his exhausting labor appears to him as a hostile force. Since alienation comes about as a result of this conflict, it is a historical reality and completely irreducible to an idea."[4] The distinction that Sartre is underscoring in Search for a Method as a whole is the distinction between *praxis*[5] and *knowledge*, but there is an additional element at work. The alienation that one experiences exists not only at the level of activity, but at the level of fundamental ontology as well. In other words, 'the given' is itself alienated, and this is experienced historically as a fact, and intellectually as ideology: "The given, which we surpass at every instant by the simple fact of living it, is not restricted to the material conditions of our existence; we must include in it, as I have said, our own childhood. What was once both a vague comprehension of our class, of our social conditioning by way of the family group, and a blind going beyond, an awkward effort to wrench ourselves away from all this, at last ends up inscribed in the form of *character*."[6] This is a significant critique of the tendency of mainstream political ideology to reify values and norms that are themselves the reflection of prior instances of politics and the structures of political economy. According to Sartre it is, ultimately, this entrenched scarcity that makes a mockery of the many discourses on values that proliferate in Capitalist societies.

Alienation then is two-fold for it exists at both the level of institutions and ideology, on the one hand, and the fundamental ontology of the given, makes the problem of knowledge and praxis unusually complex. To underscore this point, Sartre cites the example of philosophy itself. He uses the example of Kierkegaard, and cites the advancement achieved by Kierkegaard in positing "the specificity of human existence' as the focus of analysis." [7]Sartre then notes however, that the selfsame philosophy can be subjected to human agency as *alterity* and rendered as an ideology. In fact, of course, this is tantamount to a restatement of Marx's position in The German Ideology. However there is an additional point to this for Sartre, and it involves the duality of alienation: empirically experienced along the classical depiction of it by Marx: as alienation from *species, product, self, and 'Others'*; but also phenomenologically, as the 'given' that one experiences from childhood on prior to one's ability to name it, critique it, but, as 'given' one is always already in the process of surpassing it, as noted above. This is possible for Sartre because freedom is part of the Intentionality of consciousness and the later is prior to the constitution of the subject.

Because it has this dual character, alienation for Sartre means that one experiences political ideology as parasitic on 'the given'. That is to say, one experiences ideology not as the set of ideas and systems of thought that are used to maintain existing relationships of power, but as previous instances of *alterity*. Thus, for example, the "surprising" success of Right-Wing politicians and political parties is significant not only because of what this says about the current state of French or Austrian politics, for example, but also because it evinces the presence of a specific historical moment alongside of the present state of political discourse and politics, that of the history of fascism.[8] It is this duality in which the absurd or even discredited aspect of the past cohabitate the current state of political discourse that makes so much of contemporary politics, including the relationship between religion and politics, so confusing to so many. For it is not matter of the past being recalled or celebrated but of the specific historical moments coexisting as an ever present reality that can be made explicit through specific social actions. Thus the rise of Serbian nationalism which seemed so strange to observers in the West was possible because it was already part of the political culture of the Serbian nation. Its myths and narratives were not the vehicles for the readmission of nationalism into the present but were instead expressions of the past history in the present, a subtle difference, but an important one in the philosophy and praxis of social movement theory according to Sartre.

Another way of thinking about Sartre's account of social movements and alienation is to consider the duality of alienation that he says reflects the structure of bad faith. Alienation may be construed as tantamount to depicting a being that is both immanent and transcendent as immanent in its transcendence and transcendent in its immanence, and so the betrayal of the Nazi collaborator is equivalent in structure to the adoption of racist attitudes and discourses in that both involve the knowledge that the perpetrator is acting in bad faith. From a Sartrean position ignorance is not a realistic defense or justification, primarily because the knowledge of racism is a present historical moment, or is present-at-hand and adoption of it takes place with averted gaze perhaps but with awareness nevertheless. These essentialized or 'reified' categories can be constructed to pretend as in all instances of bad faith, that one is unaware of this history or that the elephant in the middle of the room does not exist, but such attempts themselves are dependent on previous ideologies of oppression and as victims of racism often point out, there is a suspiciously familiar historical sound to them. For just as the praxis of social justice against racism exists as the present-at-hand, a fact that is evinced in the re-mobilization against racism that occurs whenever racist practices and ideologies begin to proliferate; so too the ideology of racism is present-at-hand as both the practico-inert and alterity. For Sartre alienation can take on a cognitive form in which history intersects with and informs the given. Sartre provides the following illustration of the intersection of the 'given' and theory: "In 1925, when I was twenty years old, there was no chair of Marxism at the University, and communist students were very careful not to appeal to Marxism in their examinations; had they done so they would have failed. The horror of dialectic was such that Hegel himself was unknown to us. Of course, they allowed us to read Marx; they even advised us to read him; one had to know him 'in order to refute him.' But without the Hegelian tradition, without Marxist teachers, without any planned program of study, without the instruments of thought, our generation, like the preceding ones and like that which followed, was wholly ignorant of historical materialism."[9]

For Sartre then, the historical context of ideas is necessary in order to develop a clear assessment of an idea or system of ideas as either truthful or as ideology. As for Marcuse and other members of the Frankfurt School, for Sartre alienation is context dependent and human freedom is transcendental. Sartre makes this point in his discussion of 'the project': "By projecting ourselves toward our possible so as to escape the contradictions of our existence, we unveil them, and they are revealed in our very action although this action is richer than they are and gives us access to a social world in which new contradictions will involve us in new conduct. Thus we can say both that we constantly surpass our class and that our class reality is made manifest by means of this very surpassing. The realization of the possible necessarily results in the production of an object or an event in the social world; this realization is then our *objectification*, and the original contradictions which are reflected there testify to our *alienation*."[10]

So, there are two forms of alienation here, and there are two expressions of human freedom each set of which contains a primary form and one which is derivative. First-order alienation refers to the structure of consciousness itself, or one aspect of it, its bifurcation is an expression of Intentionality. There is also, however, the distinction noted throughout this analysis between freedom as an 'inescapable' fact of the Intentionality of consciousness, and the freedom whereby one selects projects, and ultimately chooses to engage in *praxis* as opposed to *alterity*. It is in this sense that the paradox of Sartre's position whereby one lives something, like alienation, before one knows it, is possible. For, one lives on the basis of the Intentionality of consciousness first, and one knows, on the basis of the constitution of the Subject, second.

We also see that in Sartre's analysis the origin of Sartre's theory of liberation on the basis of this primary state of Intentionality which includes *Mitsein* as being-for-'Others'. For, just as *Le Regard* of the other defines the world for the individual in a primordial way; so too in Search for a Method the existence of the 'Other' group, by their very presence, causes group recognition and affirmation. In a process that cannot be scripted in advance (because of the intentionality of consciousness), Sartre uses the example of the French Revolution to underscore his contention that existential freedom and contingency can give rise to a praxis of 'recognition', but not necessarily so. Sartre begins by counter-posing his position to that of mundane historicizing: "Thus, like individuals and particular enterprises, the lived falls over to the side of the irrational, the unutilizable, and the theoretician considers it to be *non-signifying*." [11]This is by now familiar criticism of the study of history within the context of a 'great narrative' of course, but it is also a critique that includes a non-critical approach to the problem of the 'reification' of history as an expression of human agency. By contrast, Sartre notes that: "Existentialism reacts by affirming the specificity of the historical event, which it refuses to conceive of as the absurd juxtaposition of a contingent residue and an *a priori* signification. Its problem is to discover a supple, patient dialectic which espouses movements as they really are and which refuses to consider *a priori* that all lived conflicts pose contradictories or even contraries. For us, *the interests* which come into play cannot necessarily find a mediation which reconciles them; most of the time they are mutually exclusive, but the fact that they cannot be satisfied at the same time does not necessarily prove that their reality is reduced to a pure contradiction of ideas." Furthermore, Sartre argues: "The day of the tenth of August, of the ninth of *Thermidor*, that day in the month of June 1848, etc., cannot be reduced to concepts. The relation between groups on each on each of those days is one of armed struggle, to be sure, and violence. But this struggle reflects *in itself* the structure of enemy groups, the immediacy insufficiently of their development, the hidden conflicts which, though never clearly declared, result in an internal disequilibrium, the deviations which the present instruments impose one each one's action, the manner in which their needs and claims are manifested to each one." [12]

As this passage underscores the fact that in order to continue the analysis of freedom and alienation we need to now introduce Sartre's concept of *praxis* and the way in which it gives rise to the expression of that freedom in social movements. This is more thematically considered in Sartre's argument in *The Critique of Dialectical Reason*. One point that he makes there is that it is also necessary to think of these social phenomena as dialectical even though dialectical thought has receded in fashion. This is especially useful when thinking through the parameters of opposition between *praxis* and *alterity* are more formally drawn.

THE POLITICS OF ABSTRACTION

It is clear from the preceding that Sartre considers the tendency of political ideology and ideology *per se* to undertake abstract analyses to be one of the major obstacles to freedom. It is such a difficult obstacle because of the relationship between epistemology and politics and in particular the tendency to ignore the political implications of epistemology let alone to consider it as a political category. Yet for Sartre gaining an understanding of the many aspects of abstraction, the faces it presents, so to speak remains a major component of radical philosophy's critique of mainstream treatment. However, what is of note in Sartre's approach to the grounding of the problem of abstraction is that his point of origin is his argument that the individual is already a being-in-the-world as intentional. For Sartre, it follows from this point of origin that the situated individual is always the most appropriate point of origin for the discussion of freedom. It is this emphasis on 'situation', about which Sartre initially wrote about in the early article on Intentionality, which is pivotal. It is so not just because represents an essential ingredient of his radical critique of ideology (from the bottom, the foundation, or the 'root,' so to speak), but also because it underscores the political agency of activity, and this includes activity that initially may appear as apolitical and of marginal significance. In other words for Sartre is an instance of abstraction to consider and then develop a discourse of individual agency without first recognizing that the individual is also acted upon by history through the present-at-hand of historical structures, ideologies and the *practico-inert*. The *practico-inert* occupies a central place in Sartre's account of history in that he views it as the basis of the class itself. He notes for example, "From this viewpoint, if the foundation of the class struggle is to lie in the *practico-inert*, this is in so far as the objective conflict of interest is both received and produced by passive activity and reveals itself in labor as a reciprocity of antagonism – possibly in a petrified form and, for example, as an exigency of the tool or machine."[13]

It may be useful in this regard to recall that Sartre stressed the Critique of Dialectical Reason that with regard to the given that the individual's existence

per se is a transcendence. It is through the initiation of *praxis* which Sartre
defines as an initial action in which the individual overcome by identifying
one's situation through reason but also through the emotions and all the other
faculties that the individual posses as a totality, since for Sartre the individual
establishes their existence as a totality anew in the project, a praxis designed
to address and overcome the scarcity-infused alterity of any situation. The action of this transcending of the given represents an implied acknowledgement
of the specific situation, in the manner in which the statement: All S are P, is
said to imply the statement: Some S are P. The answer then, to a question that
recurs throughout Sartre's phenomenology to the question: How is it possible
to live something before one knows it, is that freedom, for Sartre is defined
as a relationship to the world.[14] It is important, however, to make a distinction here. What Sartre is arguing for is not a 'third' ontology, between subject
and object, or idealism and realism, as some scholars come close to espous-
ing, but instead, a redefinition of realism as a relationship between consciousness and world, or as Intentionality.[15]

However, the situation that *praxis* overcomes is not limited to one's immediate surroundings, but also includes the socialization process as well. Sartre
underscores this point when he introduces the connection between the 'situation' of the individual and the historical context of the situation, noting that
cultural aspects of alterity can appear to take on a life of their own and then
become secondary constructs disconnected from their original historical
cause. Instead, these begin to appear as expressions of human nature through
the catch-all construct of national or ethnic character.[16] This depiction of
events culminates in the "situation" any particular individual may find themselves in and appear as an individual phenomenon where in fact it is an expression of politics mediated though culture and past moments of alterity.

Another way of saying this is that the situation is the link that Sartre establishes between the individual's existence and history, and it must be made
transparent. The situation is always infused with politics be it that of the past
or the present though ideology and such mediated phenomena as self-image
and associated phenomena such as that of one's expectations. The situation is
also a link between Sartre's existential phenomenology and the categories traditionally associated with political economy. Sartre makes class the situation
that informs praxis. As he puts it in his analysis of history, "Thus every class
is present in the other in so far as the praxis of the other tends, either directly
or through the medium of a contested object, to modify it."[17] So the situation
is not exactly an economic one, nor is it a cultural one, buts is instead a con-
textual field of past acts, institutions and cultural directives.

The Intentionality of consciousness implies that the definition of *praxis* is
transformational, since as noted it represents the attempt to transcend the

given. For Sartre it is important that the relationship between epistemology and politics is established from the outset as part of the attempt to make the political foundations of culture transparent. What Sartre refers to as a "cultural field" is such that it carries with it the biases of epistemology along with it. Thus, for example political discourses in which there are no "victims" are ones in which the political leanings of the operative epistemology have been occluded. The cultural field then presents itself as a context with its own inherent tendencies and values which quickly become entrenched as an apolitical, now cultural context.[18] For example, in the many debates over immigration that have marked the dominance of global capitalism language is presented as a cultural phenomenon that is distinct from its context in political history. So the speaking of Spanish by immigrants in the United Sates is presented as a clash of cultures without ever acknowledging the actual history through which Spanish was introduced in the American Southwest as an aspect of a political conflict. So language in this instance is not merely a cultural phenomenon but one that is reflects the practico-inert of an earlier colonial moment. A similar situation exists in Canada between the English provinces and Quebec.

Even within the cultural order the exposition of freedom needs to proceed from the *negation* of some aspect of the given, since the given is the present-at-hand of ideology as well. For although simple matter in the form of things and structures, both natural and 'socially constructed' comprise the initial element of this negation, which Sartre gives the term *pratico-inert,* it also includes more "refined" expressions including theoretical ones as well.[19] The descriptive but critical phenomenological term that Sartre uses to convey the intersection between the individual's consciousness and both coarse and "refined" expressions of the practico-inert is that of *totalization.* Totalization represents both the theoretical grasping of one's situation as well as the transformation of it through action. Furthermore, because the individual is bifurcated, one is also overcoming one's self as part of the activity of *praxis.* As Sartre notes, the actions of the individual always presuppose a context or milieu that is historical but this itself is the result of prior activities of course, but these are also present-at-hand through the practico-inert and the continuation of alterity.

Initially it would appear that this is a restriction on Sartre's idea of radical, that is intentional freedom, and a departure from the argument of *Being and Nothingness* where the exposition of freedom was such that the only restriction was on the necessity of intending a focus. However, the difference here is only one of emphasis in that the early work always included references to the Other and how the Other defines one's landscape, but now the introduction of the concepts of the practico-inert and alterity are proxies for the agency of the Other. It has always been the case that the very presence of the 'Other' defines my existential field in Being and Nothingness and that Sartre's depiction of freedom is based on the intentionality of consciousness. We can see this if we compare it with the Hobbesian notion of freedom, with its emphasis on the absence of external impediments, or with Aristotle's teleological conception of freedom where there is such great emphasis placed on the actualization of potential. Instead, for Sartre freedom begins with a 'lack'—the rupture between the for-itself and the in-itself and involves negation. So, while it is true that Sartre's emphasis is different in this later work, it is also true that the basic schema for his conception of freedom as existential is consistent through his later works: It involves the Intentionality of consciousness as its ground in both instances.

One issue that should be considered in this context is that of reification since reification appears to be a mediation between consciousness and the world. However, reification is a subset of bad faith in that it amounts to positing human freedom or a product of that freedom as an object beyond the reach of consciousness. In Sartre's later work the language of bad faith recedes but it continues to be the focus that guides his account of reification. Bad faith, in other words, resurfaces in Sartre's analysis of the relationship between ideology and 'reification'.[20]

The issue is introduced by Sartre by way of his discussion of materialism and in particular, a number of 'left critiques' of his work. On this score, Sartre notes that that "The only theory of knowledge which can be valid today is one which is founded on that truth of microphysics: the experimenter is part of the experimental system. This is the only position which allows us to get rid of the idealist illusion, the only one which shows the real man in the midst of the real world. But this realism necessarily implies a reflective point of departure; that is the *revelation* of a situation is effected in and through the *praxis* which changes it. We do not hold that this first act of becoming of the situation is the originating source of an action; we see in it a necessary moment of the action itself—the action, *in the course of its accomplishment*, provides its own clarification."[21] For Sartre this implies the Intentionality of consciousness, for without it, he argues Marx's analysis is not as powerful a critique as it can be. As he argues: "Yet the theory of knowledge continues to be a weak point in Marxism."[22] The reason for this is that, according to Sartre, in order to make the materialist case that Marx makes, one must account for the vantage point of the critical analyst. Otherwise, Sartre continues one makes the dynamic aspects of critical analysis terminate in a naturalized but abstract essence of human nature. Nor can the methodology of dialectics assist the difficulty here, for in Sartre's view the idea of consciousness as 'reflected' being is likewise problematic. Marxist epistemology is "*anti-dialectical*" in that: "When knowing is made apodictic, and when it is constituted against all possible questioning without ever defining its scope or its rights, then it is cut off from the world and becomes a formal system. When it is reduced to a pure psycho-psychological determination, it loses its primary quality, which is its relation to the object, in order to become itself a pure object of knowing. No mediation can link Marxism as a declaration of principles and apodictic truths to psycho-psychological reflection (or dialectic)."[23] The upshot of this is that for Sartre, Marx's theory of praxis has "the rudiments of a *realistic* epistemology which has never been developed."[24] Epistemology itself reflects *alienation,* and underscores the purpose of the analysis, the search for a method representing the outline for what an epistemology would need to account for in the first instance: The situated individual as being-in-the-world with all that that implies for Sartre: the coeval status of *Mit-sein,* the Intentionality of consciousness, and the emphasis on agency, or as Sartre now refers to it, *praxis.*

One significant category that Sartre introduces to his exposition of 'realism' is the formulation of a conception of 'realism' according to which one's experience is mediated not only by individual 'Others' but by groups as well. The reason why this is significant is that it introduces the idea of multiple identities into Sartre's social theory. This is not to say that this is a major point of emphasis in Sartre's work, however, it is the case that there is the basis in Sartre's social theory for the exposition of such a philosophy. These groups 'check' or mediate one's field just as the individual did in the previous works, and one is neither 'this or that' identity alone, but instead an ensemble of identities each of which exert pressure on the individual. It may be useful in this regard to say a word about Sartre's theory of ensembles. The creation of an ensemble has always been treated as a mysterious phenomena whether it occurs in the performing arts or in the politics of mass movements. Sartre's perspective contains elements of the earlier contributions of Aristotle and Hegel but also Marx and the socialist tradition. For example, he follows Aristotle in noting the distinction between an unorganized totality and a unity one. In order for a disorganized collective or aggregate to unify there must be a crisis of some sort. Here, Sartre agrees with the majority of social movement theorists who focus on a catalyst in the form of a grievance as a necessary spark for united action. Such an occurrence may lead to a spontaneous job action or it may only contribute to a greater sense of crisis among those who are directly influenced by it. This is because for Sartre the opportunity to not act remains an existential possibility throughout the life of a social movement. In fact, at this juncture, especially in liberal societies where the emphasis is so heavily placed on finding individual solutions, it is quite possible that after the initial crisis individuals may seek to find individual solutions to what is in fact a social or political problem and crisis. The next step involves continued organizing through the pressures exerted by both the *practico-inert* and the overall condition of scarcity. Here something like a closed factory, or the issuance of a subpoena might serve as the practico-inert as noted earlier. The ensuing overall clarification of demands that takes place may in itself serve as a critique of the context within which the immediacy of the practico-inert, as an exigency with a *telos*, exerts itself. A new consciousness at this point is born and it is an historical consciousness but it is one that remains existential along the lines laid out by Hegel in his description of the "unhappy consciousness." The creation of an ensemble takes place through the unhappy consciousness and in it the individual and group are synthesized temporarily in a group-as-one or the *group en fusion*. At this point the disorganized assembly of individuals that we began with no longer exists and a new social ontology has been temporarily created. It is important to note that for Sartre this is a contingent state of affairs from start to finish. This is why, for example, after the end of the Vietnam War it was so difficult for movement organizers to maintain any form of social cohesion for further political change. It was not merely that the goal, the end of the Vietnam War, had been realized, but rather that the reality of individual consciousness reasserted itself. In other words, the convocation of subjectivities that existed during the time of the social movement no longer held and so along with its dispersal came the reversion of these subjectivities back to their original state which is, once again, the priority of consciousness over subjectivity and individual consciousness at that. Social and mass movements involve the creation of new subjectivities and only then the creation of new identities and so the appearance of social movement subjectivity is an unusual occurrence and not the ordinary state of affairs. This is the legacy of Sartre's early theory of consciousness and intentionality which now reappears in his theory of practical ensembles and praxis.

We can see this more nuanced approach in the illustration that Sartre provides: "It is clear, in fact, that the factory worker is subject to the pressure of his 'production group,' but if, as is the case at Paris, he lives rather far from his place of work, he is equally subject to the pressure of his 'residential group.' Now these groups exert various actions upon their members; sometimes, even, the particular 'block,' the 'housing project,' the 'neighborhood' checks in each person the impetus given by the factory or the shop."[25]

Each of these associations entails a different form of subjective, or derived activity and identity, and yet, by the same token, each set of identities is informed by different expressions of the practico-inert. Only a particular type of subjectivity, that of the group-en-fusion will establish the kind of sweeping social demands that one sees in truly revolutionary mass movements. For example, during the mobilization of the Solidarity Movement in Poland, the shipyard in Gdansk, Poland represented a type of identity but it was only when that identity gave rise to another subjectivity, that of Polish resistance, that the practico-inert of the shipyard itself became a political venue for resistance. It is not that the political implications of the shipyard had been latent, for the politics of alienation was present-at-hand to the Polish workers all along. What changed and what revealed the practico-inert as such was the convocation of subjectivities that is represented by progressive adumbrations of praxis coupled with the emergence of the group-en-fusion and the radical change in identity from one that was immersed in the present to one which had historical roots.

'SARTRE'S LATER THEORY OF RECOGNITION'

In his later work Sartre is far more explicitly focused on the political component of 'recognition' than he was in Being and Nothinness, where 'the look' held such prominence. It will be recalled however that in the earlier concept of being-for-Others, although it posits a universe of 'Others,' it was usually a matter of this particular 'Other' that was Sartre's primary concern. The difference in emphasis between the early and late works reflects his different intent in the case of the later works Sartre is locating his concept of intentionality within a political philosophy which for Sartre always implied class analysis.[26] However, the difference also reflects the influence of dialectics in the *Critique of Dialectical Reason*. For, it is part and parcel of dialectical methodology to focus on the opposition of, essentially, groups and not individuals. That is to say, it is particularly suited to the levels of analysis that correspond to aggregates—the group, the class, the nation, or history itself. Thus, it is important to remember that the starting point for Sartre's analysis was not that of the aggregate, but of the individual, and the Intentionality of consciousness. So, the *Critique of Dialectical Reason* is less a departure from phenomenology as it is a different area of focus.[27] Certain aspects of one's *praxis* may not be immediately discernable owing to the influence of history on culture. This is a point noted by Kruks in her discussion of the constituted dialectic: "This is a dialectic in which *praxis* is no longer open to immediate comprehension by individual agents. Its opacity arises from the fact that it is not a dialectic of individual *praxis*, but a dialectic of ensembles."[28] In a sense, Sartre extends his relational ontology to groups which oppose each other: "Inasmuch as each revealed activity of a group surpasses the activity of an opposing group, is modified in its tactics because of the latter and consequently modifies the structures of the group itself, the event in its full concrete reality is the organized unity of a plurality of oppositions reciprocally surpassed."[29] An illustration might serve to make this point clearer. During the movement for civil rights in the U.S. during the 1960s civil rights activists routinely encountered a change in tactics by the institutions of white supremacy: Local Courts, police officials, as well as, of course, in some instances, elected officials, such as allowing only one or two protesters to march at a time, or mass arrests. This change in tactics by local police departments necessitated a change in tactics by organizers, who responded, for example, by having children march. This particular tactic, coming as it did at the beginning of modern news coverage, underscored the dissonance between the violence of the institutions and culture of white supremacy, even while allowing adult activists to remain active and, more to the point, out of jail for future organized events. Social movement tactics are continually changing as result of the opposition of the *praxis* of groups. However, it is important to note that this change in tactics in inconceivable without the concept and reality of 'recognition' as a basis for it.

Thus, the existence of 'recognition' can be posited negatively as reaction. It also exists positively in the *group-in-fusion*. However, as Kruks notes, for Sartre, that "is possible only in exceptional circumstances."[30] There is instead, a more everyday experience of affirming 'recognition' and that is termed by Sartre *reciprocity*.[31] Kruks notes this point in the discussion of *scarcity*: "Reciprocity, like being-for-Others', remains a *dyadic* relation of mutual recognition."[32] Reciprocity establishes that *praxis* itself becomes a secondary form of recognition, for it is "synthetically enriched because the praxis of each of us is the same."[33] This particular dialectic in which the individual recognizes a similarity of *praxis* and then acts to realize change involves the explication of Sartre's social theory which not the area of focus here. Our purpose in raising the issue of mutuality of *praxis* was to underscore the place of recognition in Sartre's later work.

We can see certain aspects of the theory of recognition if we reflect on Sartre's earlier study of Anti-Semitism. For Sartre the template for anti-Semitism is bad faith, and so bad faith is a political category simply by dint of the fact that it concerns the Other. However, for Sartre anti-Semitism has at its core a pronounced fear of the human condition: "We are now in a position to understand the anti-Semite. He is a man who is afraid."[34] This seems a bit too pat, except that it is essential to recall that for Sartre the capacity to negate and to even take a negative stance towards one's self is part of the primordial state of being-in-the-world. So anti-Semitism is a substitute for the acknowledgement of one's power to self-negation. So when we ask what exactly it is that the anti-Semite is afraid of, Sartre's response is that it is existence itself. In fact, the anti-Semite is afraid of everything except the Jew: "Of himself, of his own consciousness, of his liberty, of his instincts, of his responsibilities, of solitariness, of change, of society, and of the world—of everything except the Jews."[35] But what afflicts the anti-Semite is not just fear but bad faith. He desires to become an object, an entity among entities "who does not simply adopt an opinion, he chooses himself as a person. He chooses the permanence and impenetrability of stone. . ."[36] In his early analysis of the topic anti-Semitism is an instance of bad faith, and as an instance, it is interchangeable with other instances of bad faith: "The Jew serves him only as a pretext. . . The existence of the Jew merely permits the anti-Semite to stifle his anxieties at their inception by persuading himself that his place in the world has been marked out in advance, that it awaits him, and that tradition gives him the right to occupy it. Anti-Semitism, in short, is fear of the human condition. The anti-Semite is a man who wishes to be a pitiless stone, a furious torrent, a devastating thunderbolt—anything except a man."[37] If one prefers, it is a Sartrean version of the Freudian theory of transference.

    If we return to the level of social movement analysis we can see that the concept of bad faith remains an essential one for Sartre's later theory of recognition. For whereas in the earlier study of anti-Semitism we saw that for Sartre there was a deliberate attempt to destroy by dis-recognition or negation *this particular Jew*; in his later work the politics works from a social level. In the earlier work for he example, Sartre criticizes the so-called democrat because he or she denies individuation, he notes, "The democrat, like the scientist, fails to see the particular case; to him the individual is only an ensemble of individual traits. It follows that his defense of the Jew saves the latter as man and annihilates him as Jew."[38] However, if we reflect on anti-Semitism from the perspective of the theory of the practico-inert the prior history of anti-Semitism is a structure that is present-at-hand through the reestablishment of anti-Semitic languages and structures.[39]

CONCLUSION

The theory of recognition that Sartre illustrated in his literary and philosophical works throughout his early and middle period evinced an unusual sensitivity to the directness of the human encounter with reality. 'Others' were part of this encounter but the emphasis remained on the directness of the human experience of being-in-the-world. In other words, the view of recognition that one finds in Sartre's early and middle works is one wherein recognition is presented from the perspective of present consciousness for that is the point at which consciousness and the world intersect. In his later works, beginning with the Condemned of Altona, Sartre begins to consider the historical ground of consciousness. The major philosophical work of the period, the Critique of

Dialectical Reason is still an exposition of philosophy from the vantage point of being-in-the-world as a phenomenon thoroughly informed by the intentionality of consciousness, even if it is political philosophy and even if it uses class analysis. This is due in part to the fact that Sartre's analysis od social and political reality departs from most accounts of causality in political philosophy and if one asks why the answer lies in the structure of consciousness worked out by Sartre in his very first philosophical works. Sartre's view of political causality is radical because his concept of intentionality is radical, for it simply will not settle for anything other than the deepest and fullest explanation of political reality. His critique of the various schools after all, be they structuralism, traditional Marxist analysis, liberal democratic theory or even behaviorism, is not so much that these perspectives contain outright falsifications but that by stopping so far short of the mark, and thereby by presenting the mediated cause of political reality as the most rational one, they yield a second order series of discourses, some of which become stand alone ideologies. Sartre's radicalism is two-fold for it consists not only in the fact that the point of origin for it is human activity in situ or praxis, but that praxis itself is part of an historical activity in which social praxis confronts the condition of scarcity as both an individual challenge, for praxis remains an existential, contingent category, and a social or group one in which the alienation of social structures and ideologies from the past is experience as the present-at-hand of the practico-inert.

   The full weight of Sartre's radicalism truly emerges when one tries to think through the implications of his philosophy in the political order. This appeared perhaps in its clearest form in his Preface to Wretched of the Earth but it is present whenever one takes his account of reality seriously. If one inquires about the causes of any human choice one may find that in fact a behavioral explanation fits quite nicely but if we inquire as Sartre's works insists that we do and think more deeply we may want to ask about the behavioral motivations themselves and why it, for example, that individuals respond so predictably but significantly, *not universally*, to behavioral cues. Viewed slightly differently, one might say of contemporary American society and increasingly of the West, that recognition has been reduced to the lowest common denominator and that the obsession with individuation that one sees everywhere is what Americans have chosen to do with their freedom of choice. Yet Sartre would have us ask about the function these achievements mask in terms of authenticity and existential freedom. Freedom of choice in other words can just as easily be pressed into the service of bad faith as any other human endeavor. These expressions of pseudo-recognition are precisely a denial of the kind of genuine encounter and recognition that occurs whenever the *group-en-fusion* comes into being. Finally, it may be said that the *group-en-fusion* is a social category in that the mutual recognition it fosters establishes recognition, viewed as a human need from Rousseau onwards, that is an existentialist approach to the basic problem of the politics of existence, the condition of scarcity itself.

NOTES

1. Jean Paul-Sartre, *Anti-Semite and Jew,* (New York: Schochen Books, 1995): p. 69.

2. Jean-Paul Sartre, *The Critique of Dialectical Reason* (New York: Verso, 2004): 715

3. Jean-Paul Sartre, *Search for a Method,* (New York: Vantage, 1968): 91.

4. Ibid.: 13-14.

5. *Praxis,* as Sartre uses it, refers to human agency directed toward the affirmation, as opposed to the negation, of human existence. Its negative form is given the term, *alterity.* On this topic Richard Bernstein's classical distinction between practice and praxis remains pivotal.

6. Ibid.: 100-101.

7. Ibid.: 12.

8. Fascism defined here as a political ideology in which tradition is invoked for the purpose 'recognizing' one group in society at the expense, or by 'negating' another. While there are many other definitions of fascism that one can cite, the core element as far Sartre's critique of it exposited in Being and Nothingness is the element of 'recognition'.

9. Sartre, op. cit., 1968: 17.

10. Ibid.: 101.

11. Ibid.: 126.

12. Ibid: 127.

13. Sartre, op. cit., 2004: 713

14. Sartre notes this point in *Being and Nothingness* in the course of his depiction of an 'ontological proof' during which he notes that the issue involves not epistemology, but instead, ontology.

15. Sonia Kruks (New York: Unwin Hyman, 1990).

16. Ibid., 144.

17. Sartre, op. cit., 2004: 710.

18. Included in this is such seemingly unrelated and essentially apolitical categories as aesthetics. Aesthetic values are located in a cultural context, of this even the most conservative theorist would assent. However, Sartre is insistent that this context itself be rendered transparent though the delineation of cultural history. When accomplished in this way aesthetics appears as the present-at-hand in cultural form, of prior instances of politics.

19. *Praxis* also creates new social structures and objects, of course, and these themselves become the new expressions of practico-inert that must be transcended by the individual.

20. One could, by way of underscoring just how persistent the problem of 'reification' is, cite the very passage where political philosophy first addresses this issue: "The Allegory of the Cave" in Plato's Republic. For, although 'reification' as the reification of 'consciousness' is a modern problem, as a problem, perhaps even the problem of politics. For Plato the solution to alienation must involve leadership, a position echoed by Rousseau in his depiction of the lawgiver. However what is left unanswered by Plato is precisely how it is that one of the prisoners, chained since childhood, manages to effect a transformation in the human condition from one of alienation to one of liberation.

21. Sartre, op. cit., 32.

22. Ibid.

23. Ibid.

24. Ibid., 32.

25. Sartre, op. cit., 1968: 66.

26. The view that Sartre "discovered" class as a political category in his later works is seriously mistaken. His early works including are heavily imbued with class analysis. Furthermore, his extended responses to Left critiques of his works evince a clear knowledge of class theory. The difficulty seems to be that the concepts that he uses in his later works are more specifically associated with class analysis.

27. This is not to say that phenomenology is ill-suited to the study of more universal levels of analysis, but that dialectical exposition, with its emphasis on opposition, is more directly suited to depicting the rationality of class analysis.

28. Kruks, op. cit.,: 155.

29. Sartre, op. cit.,:128

30. Kruks, op. cit., : 154

31. Ibid: 167

32. Ibid.

33. Ibid., p. 170

34. Sartre, op. cit., 1948: 53

35. Ibid.: 53.

36. Ibid.

37. Ibid.: 54

38. Ibid.: 56

39. The two-fold directionality of anti-Semitism involves the connection to historical instances in both cases of course. However, at the level of the nation-state the attempt is first of all to inflict on individuals through the social category a direction towards self-alienation and negation. Thus, for example, when the leader of a nation-state denies the reality of the holocaust, it is more than a negation of a group, it is a removal of recognition and thereby a negation of individuals as well.

Bibliography

Abra, Jock. "Existential Approaches II: Jean Paul Sartre," in *Assaulting Parnassus: Theoretical Views of Creativity*. Lanham, MD: University Press of America, 1988.

Allan, George. "Sartre's Constriction of the Marxist Dialect." *Review of Metaphysics* 33 (1979):87-108.Reprinted with the permission of the Catholic University America.

Arendt, Hannah. *The Life of the Mind*. Harcourt Brace Jovanovich, Inc. Orlando, Florida, 1978.

Aronson, Ronald. " Sartre and the Dialectic: The Purpose of *Critique, II*." From the book: *Existentialist Politics and Political Theory*. Series: Sartre and Existentialism: Philosophy, Politics, Ethics, The psyche, Literature, and Aesthetics. By William L. McBride. Garland Publishing, Inc., New York & London, 1997.

Anderson, Thomas. "The Obligation to Will the Freedom of Others According to Jean-Paul Sartre," in Dallery, Arleen and others Eds. *The Question of the Other: Essays in Contemporary Continental Philosophy*. Albany: SUNY Press, 1989.

Atlas, Jeffrey. "Concepts of History and Ideology in Historical Dialectics." *Dialectical Anthropology*. 12(4) 421-434, 1987.

Atwood, George. "Psychoanalytic Phenomenology and the Thinking of Martin Heidegger And Jean Paul Sartre" in Detrick, Douglas and Detrick, Susan Ed. *Self Psychology: Comparisons and Contrasts*. Hillsdale: Analytic Press, 1989.

Audi, Robert ed. Cambridge Dictionary of Philosophy. Cambridge: Cambridge University Press, 1999

Barnes, Hazel. "Sartre on the Emotions." In *Sartre and Existentialism: Philosophy, Politics, Ethics, The psyche, Literature, and Aesthetics*. By William L. McBride. Garland Publishing, Inc., New York & London, 1997.

———, " Sartre's Ontology: The Revealing and Making of Being." In Existentialist Ontology and Human Consciousness. Series: *Sartre and Existentialism*: Philosophy, Politics, Ethics, The psyche, Literature, and Aesthetics. By William L. McBride. Garland Publishing, Inc., New York & London, 1997.

Baugh, Bruce. "Sartre and James on the Role of the Body in Emotion." In *Existentialist Ontology and Human Consciousness.*

Bernstein, Jay M. Adorno: *Disenchantment and Ethics*. New York: Cambridge University Press, 2001.

Bernstein, Richard J. " From Hermeneutics to Praxis." In *Hermeneutics and Praxis* by Robert Hollinger, University of Notre Dame Press. Notre Dame, Indiana 1985.

———, "Philosophy in the Conversation of Mankind." From the book: Hermeneutics and Praxis by Robert Hollinger, University of Notre Dame Press. Notre Dame, Indiana 1985.

———, "Hannah Arendt: The Ambiguities of Theory and Practice," in Terrence Ball ed. *Political Theory and Practice*: New Perspectives. Minneapolis: University of Minnisota Press, 1977.

Birt, Robert. "Alienation in the Later Philosophy of Jean-Paul Sartre," *Man and World*, 19(3): 293 -309, 1986

———. "The Prospects for Community in the Later Sartre," *International Philosophical Quarterly.* 29(2): 139-148, 1989.

Bukala C. "Jean Paul Sartre: A Topical Bibliography," *Review of Existential Psychology and Psychiatry* 13 (1): 106-124, 1974

Butler, Judith. "Sartre: The Imaginary Pursuit of Being," in Butler, *Subjects of Desire: Hegelian Reflections in Twentieth Century France.* New York: Columbia, 1987.

Cahn, Steven M., Kitcher, Patricia & Sher, George. *Reason at Work: Introductory Readings in Philosophy.* Harcourt Brace Jovanovich, Inc., Orlando, Florida, 1984.

Caputo, John D. *Heidegger and Aquinas: An Essay on Overcoming Metaphysics.* New York, Fordham University Press, 1982.

———, "Heidegger's Original Ethics" New Scholasticism Vol. 45 Winter 1971 "Being, Sound and Play in Heidegger" *Man & World* Vol. 3

———, *The Mystical Element in Heidegger*, Fordham University Press,1986. " The Thought of Being and the Conversation of Mankind: The case of Heidegger and Rorty." In *Hermeneutics and Praxis* by Robert Hollinger, University of Notre Dame Press. Notre Dame, Indiana 1985.

Cannon, Betty." The Death of the Objective Observer: Sartre's Dialectical Reason as an Epistemology for the Social Sciences. "*Man and World* 18(1985):269-93.

Carr, David. *Phenomenology and the Problem of History.* Evanston: Northwestern University Press, 1974.

Catalano, Joseph. "Authenticity: A Sartrean Perspective," *Philosophical Forum*, 22(2), Winter, 1990/1991.

———,*Good Faith and Other Essays.* Rowman & Littlefield Publishers, Inc., Lanham, Maryland 1996.

Contat, Michel and Rybalka, Michel. The Writings of Jean Paul Sartre, Vol.1. Evanston: Northwestern University Press, 1974.

DeBeauvoir, Simone. "Merleau-Ponty and Pseudo-Sartreanism," in Jon Stewart ed. *The Debate Between Sartre and Merleau-Ponty.* Evanston: Northwestern, 1998.

Detmer, David. *Freedom as a Value.* La Salle: Open Court, 1986.

Derrida, Jacques. "Ousia and Gramme: A Note to a Footnote in Being and Time,"

Edward Casey trans., in *Phenomenology in Perspective*, Smith, ed. The Hague: Nijhoff, 1970.

Desan, Wilfrid. "An English Version of Sartre's Main Philosophical Work: Critique of Dialectical Reason." *Philosophy Today* 24(Fall 1980):262-71.Reprinted with the permission of *Philosophy Today*.

——, "Sartre the Individualist."*In patterns of the Life-world: Essays in Honor of John Wild*, edited by James M. Edie, Francis H. Parker , and Calvin O. Schrag. Evanston: Northwestern University Press, 1970

Douglas, Kanneth. *A Critical Bibliography of Existentialism* (the Paris School, Listing Books and Articles in English and French by and About Jean-Paul Sartre, Simone de Beauvoir, Maurice Merleau-Ponty). New Haven: Yale French Studies, 1950

Dreyfus, Hubert L. "Holism and Hermeneutics." In *Hermeneutics and Praxis* by Robert Hollinger, University of Notre Dame Press. Notre Dame, Indiana 1985.

D'Souza, Dinish. *The End of Racism*. New York: The Free Press, 1996.

Eagleton, Terry & Milne, Drew. *Marxist literary Theory: A Reader*. Blackwell Publishers Ltd. Oxford, UK, 1996.

Edie M., James. "The question of the Transcendental Ego: Sartre's Critique of Husserl."

Existentialist Ontology and Human Consciousness. Series: *Sartre and Existentialism: Philosophy, Politics, Ethics, The psyche, Literature, and Aesthetics*. By William L. McBride. Garland Publishing, Inc., New York & London, 1997.

Erickson, John. "Sartre's African Writings: Literature and Revolution." *L'Esprit Createur* 10 (1970):182-96.

Eyerman, Ron and Andrew Jamison eds. *Social Movements: A Cognitive Approach*. Penn State: Penn State Press, 1991.

Flynn, Thomas R. " Epistemology and Politics in the Later Sartre." In *Existentialist Politics and Political Theory*. Series: Sartre and Existentialism: Philosophy, Politics, Ethics, The psyche, Literature, and Aesthetics. By William L. McBride. Garland Publishing, Inc., New York & London, 1997.

——, Thomas. Sartre, Foucault, and Historical Reason. 1998

Fraser, Nancy. "What's Critical About Critical Theory." In *Feminist Interpretations and Political Theory*. Mary Lyndon Shanley ed. State College: Penn State Press, 1991.

Freud, Sigmund. *Civilization and its Discontents*. New York: W.W. Norton, 1962

Fromm, Eric. *Beyond the Chains of Illusion; My Encounter With Marx and Freud*. NewYork: Simon and Schuster, 1962.

——, *Escape from Freedom*. New York: Anchor, 1968.

Foucault, Michel. "About the Beginnings of the Hermeneutics of the Self; Two Lectures at Dartmouth." Mark Blasius ed., in *Political Theory*, vol.21, no.2, May 1993.

Frenkel-Brunswick, Else, Daniel J Levinson, Theodor Wiesengrund Adorno and R. Nevitt Sanford. *The Authoritarian Personality*. New York: W.W. Norton, 1993.

Fucicello, Theresa. *Tyranny of Kindness*. New York: Atlantic Monthly Press, 1994.

Gillian, Garth Jackson. "A Question of Method: History and Critical Experience." *In Jean-Paul Sartre: Contemporary Approaches to His Philosophy*, edited by Hugh J. Silverman and Frederick A. Elliston (Pittsburgh: Duquesne University Press, 1980); 141-54.

Gerwitsch, Arron. Phenomenology and the Modern World, in *Hermeneutics and Praxis*. South Bend: University of Notre Dame Press, 1985.

Hegel, G. W. F. Lectures on the *History of Philosophy*: Greek Philosophy

—— , *The Phenomenology of Mind*. New York: Harper, 1967.

—— , *Reason in History*: A General Introduction to the philosophy of History. Tr. Robert S. Hartman. The Bobbs-Merrill Company, Inc., Indianapolis, New York 1953.

Heidegger, Martin. *Being and Time*. Tr. John Macquarrie & Edward Robinson. Harper. & Row, Publishers, Inc., New York, NY, 1962

—— , Early Greek Thinking. Tr. David Farrell and Frank A. Capuzzi. Harper & Row, Publisher, Inc., New York, 1984.

Hobbes, Thomas. *Leviathan*. The Bobbs-Merrill Company, Inc., Indianapolis, New York 1958.

Hollinger, Robert. *Hermeneutics and Praxis*. University of Notre Dame Press, Notre Dame, Indiana, 1985.

Husserl, Edmund. *The Crisis of the European Sciences*. Tr. David Carr. Evanston: Northwestern, 1970

—— . *Ideas*. Boyce Gibson, TR. New York: Allen & Unwin, 1952.

—— . Kersten tr. Boston: Nijhoff, 1980.

—— . *Philosophy as Rigorous Science* Tr. Quentin Lauer. In *Phenomenology and the Crisis of Philosophy*. New York: Harper, 1965

—— . *"Phenomenology and the Crisis of Modern Man,"* Tr. Quentin Lauer. In Ingram, David. " Hermeneutics and Truth. " In *Hermeneutics and Praxis* by Robert Hollinger, University of Notre Dame Press. Notre Dame, Indiana 1985.

Jaspers, Karl. *Philosophy Volume 2*. Tr. E.B. Ashton. The University of Chicago Press. Chicago and London, 1970.

Kierkegaard, Soren. *Fear and Trembling*. Tr. Alastair Hannay. New York: Viking, 1986.

—— , *The Sickness Unto Death*. Howard V. Hony ed. Princeton: Princeton University Press.

Kirk, G.S., Raven, J.E. & Schofield, M. *The Presocratic Philosophers*. Cambridge University Press, Cambridge, UK, 1983.

Kisiel, Theodore. " The Happening of Tradition: The Hermeneutics of Gadamer and Heidegger." *Hermeneutics and Praxis* by Robert Hollinger, University of Notre Dame Press. Notre Dame, Indiana 1985.

Kruks, Sonia. *Situation and Human Existence*. New York: Unwin Hyman, 1990

Langer, Monika. "Sartre and Marxist Existentialism." In *Existentialist Politics and Political Theory*. Series: Sartre and Existentialism: Philosophy, Politics, Ethics, The psyche, Literature, and Aesthetics. By William L. McBride. Garland Publishing, Inc., New York & London, 1997.

Lapointe, François. "Supplement to Bibliography on Jean-Paul Sartre," *Man and World* 14(1): 77-100, 1981

Lauer, Quentin. *Essays in Hegelian Dialectic*. New York: Fordham, 1977.

Leak, Andrew. *Sartre*. New York: Reaktion Books, 2006.

Lessing, Arthur. "Marxist Existentialism. " *Review of Metaphysics* 20 (1967):461-82.

Levin, David. *Reason and Evidence in Husserl's Phenomenology*. Evanston: Northwestern University Press, 1970

Levinas, Emmanuel. *The Theory of Intuition in Husserl's Phenomenology*. Evanston Northwestern University Press, 1973.

Levy, Bernard Henri and Andrew Brown. *Sartre: Philosopher of the Twentieth-Century*. Cambridge, U.K.: Polity, 2003

Liebman, Stuart and Enzo Traverso. "The Blindness of the Intellectuals, Historicizing Sartre's Anti-Semite and Jew," *October Magazine*, 87, (1999), via Ebsco.

Lukacs, Georg. *History and Class Consciousness*. Tr. R. Livingston. Cambridge: MIT Press, 1976.

Mansfield, Harvey. *Manliness*. New Haven: Yale, 2006.

Marcuse, Herbert. *Between Luther and Popper*. New York: Verso, 1983.

—— , 'Existentialism: Remarks on Jean-Paul Sartre's *L'Etre et Le Neant*." In *Existentialist Ontology and Human Consciousness*. Series: Sartre and Existentialism: Philosophy, Politics, Ethics, The psyche, Literature, and Aesthetics. By William L. McBride. Garland Publishing, Inc., New York & London, 1997.

Marks, Carol. "Sartre and the Jews: A Felicitous Misunderstanding," *October Magazine*, 87, (1999), via Ebsco

—— , and Pierre Birnbaum. ""Sorry Afterthoughts on Anti-Semite and Jew," *October Magazine*, 87, (1999) via Ebsco.

Martinot, Steve. "L' Esprit Objectif as a Theory of Language. " *Man and World* 26 (1992):45-62.

Marx, Karl. *Capital*. New York: International, 1977.

—— , "Estranged Labor." *The Economic and Philosophical Manuscripts of 1844*. Dirk Struik ed. New York: International: 1978.

Mazis, Glen A. "A new Approach to Sartre's Theory of Emotions." In *Existentialist Ontology and Human Consciousness*. Series: Sartre and Existentialism: Philosophy, Politics, Ethics, The psyche, Literature, and Aesthetics. By William L. McBride. Garland Publishing, Inc., New York & London, 1997.

McBride, William L. "Sartre and Marxism." *Existentialist Politics and Political Theory*. Series: *Sartre and Existentialism: Philosophy, Politics, Ethics, The Psyche, Literature, and Aesthetics*. By William L. McBride. Garland Publishing, Inc., New York & London, 1997.

—— , "Existentialist Ontology and Human Consciousness". Series: *Sartre and Existentialism: Philosophy, Politics, Ethics, The psyche, Literature, and Aesthetics*. Garland Publishing, Inc., New York & London, 1997.

McCulloch, Gregory. *Using Sartre*. Routledge: London, 1994.

Merleau-Ponty, Maurice. *The Phenomenology of Perception*. Colin Smith tran. London: Routledge, 1962.

Misgeld, Dieter. " On Gadamer's Hermeneutics." In *Hermeneutics and Praxis* by Robert Hollinger, University of Notre Dame Press. Notre Dame, Indiana 1985.

Moreland, James. "For-Itself and In-Itself in Sartre and Merleau-Ponty," *The Debate Between Sartre and Merleau-Ponty.* Jon Stewart ed. Evanston: Northwestern, 1998.

Mulhall, Stephen. *Routledge Guide to Heidegger and Being and Time.* New York: Routledge,1996

Ollman, Bertell. *Alienation; Marx's Concept of Man in Capitalist Society.* Cambridge: Cambridge University Press, 1978.

Paci, Enzo. " Practico-Inert Praxis and Irreversibility ." *In the Function of the Sciences and the Meaning of Man.* Translated by Paul Piccone and James E. Hansen (Evanston: Northwestern University Press, 1971):347-70.Reprinted with the permission of Northwestern University Press.

Petrey, Sandy. "Reflections on the Goyishe Question," *October Magazine,* 87, (1999).

Plato. *The Republic.* Tr. Francis MacDonald Cornford. New York: Oxford,1991

Poster, Mark. *Existential Marxism in postwar France: From Sartre to Althusser.* Princeton University press, Princeton, New Jersey 1975.

Roelofs, H. Mark *The Poverty of American Politics.* Philadelphia: Temple University Press, 1998.

Rorty, Richard. " Postmodernist Bourgeois Liberalism." In *Hermeneutics and Praxis* by Robert Hollinger. South Bend: University of Notre Dame Press, 1985.

Rousseau, Jean Jacques. *The Social Contract.* Tr. Charles Frankel. Hafner Publishing Company, New York, 1957.

Ryhalka, Michel. Jean-Paul Sartre: A Selected General Bibliography," in Schilpp, Paul Ed.*The Philosophy of Jean-Paul Sartre.* Las Salle, IL: Open Court, 1981, 709-729

Sample, Ruth. *Exploitation.* New York: Rowmen and Littlefield, 2003.

Sartre, Jean–Paul. *Anti-Semite and Jew.* Tr. George. J. Becker. Shocken Books, Inc. New York, NY, 1962.

——— , *Being and Nothingness:* An Essay on Phenomenological Ontology. Tr. Hazel E. Barnes. Washington Square Press, New York, 1966.

——— , *Critique de la Raison Dialectique.* Gallimard, Paris, 1960

——— , *Critique of Dialectical Reason,* (Vol. 1 & 2). Verso, New York, 2004-6

——— , "Intentionality, A fundamental Idea of Husserl's Phenomenology," Translator, Joseph P. Fell. *Journal of the British Society for Phenomenology,* 1, 1970.

——— , "Merleau-Ponty *Vivan,t*" in Jon Stewart ed. *The Debate Between Sartre and Merleau-Ponty.* Evanston: Northwestern, 1998.

——— , *Nausea.* New York: New Directions, 1964.

——— , *No exit & The Files.* TR. Stuart Gilbert. Alfred A. Knopf, Inc., New York, NY, 1946.

——— , *Search for a Method.* Vantage, New York, 1968.

——— , *Transcendence of the Ego.* New York: Farrar, Straus and Giroux, 1991.

Schoolman, Morton. *The Imaginary Witness; The Critical Theory of Herbert Marcuse.* New York: The Free Press, 1980.

Schor, Naomi. "Anti-Semitism, the Jews and the Universal," *October Magazine,* 87 (1999).

Bibliography 129

Schrag, Calvin O. *The Self After Postmodernity*. New Haven: Yale University Press, 1999.
Shepley, John. "The Intellectual as Jew, Sartre Against McCarthyism: An Unfinished Play," *October Magazine*, 87 (1999), via the Internet from Ebsco.
Sheridan, James F. "On Ontology and Politics: A Polemic," in Jon Stewart ed. *The Debate Between Sartre and Merleau-Ponty*. Evanston: Northwestern, 1998.
Sherover, Charles M. *The Human Experience of Time: The Development of Its Philosophic Meaning*. New York: New York University Press 1975.
Simont, Juliette . "The Critique of Dialectical Reason: From Need to Need, Circularly." Translated by Thomas Trezise. *Yale French Studies* 68(1985):108-23.
Stern, Alfred. *Sartre: His Philosophy and Existential Psychoanalysis*. Dell. Publishing Co., Inc., New York, 1967.
Stack, George J. "Sartre's Dialectics of Social Relations. " *Philosophy and Phenomenological research* 31(1971):394-408.
Stewart, Jon.ed. *The Debate Between Sartre and Merleau-Ponty*. Evanston: Northwestern, 1998.
——— , "Philosophy and Political Engagement: Letters from the Quarrel Between Sartre andMerleau-Ponty".
Suleiman, Susan. "Rereading Rereading: Further Reflections on Sartre's Reflexions," *October Magazine*, 87 (1999), from the Internet via Ebsco.
Tarrow, Sidney. *Power in Movement: Social Movements and Contentious Politics*. New York: Cambridge University Press, 1998.
Vidal-Naquiet, Pierre. "Remembrances of a 1946 Reader," Tr. Denis Hollier and Rosalind Krauss, *October Magazine*, 87 (1999), via Ebsco.
Warnock, Mary. " Imagination in Sartre." In *Existentialist Ontology and Human Consciousness*. Series: Sartre and Existentialism: Philosophy, Politics, Ethics, The psyche, Literature, and Aesthetics. By William L. McBride. Garland Publishing, Inc., New York & London, 1997.
Waltzer, Michael. "Preface to the New Edition" of *Anti-Semite and Jew*. Tr. George Becker New York: Schocken Books, 1995.
Wider, Kathleen. "The Failure of Self- Consciousness in Sartre's *Being and Nothingness*." In Existentialist Ontology and Human Consciousness. Series: Sartre and Existentialism: Philosophy, Politics, Ethics, The psyche, Literature, and Aesthetics. By William L. McBride. Garland Publishing, Inc., New York & London, 1997.

Index